*While we look not at the things which are seen,*
*but at the things which are not seen:*
*for the things which are seen are temporal;*
*but the things which are not seen are eternal.*
2 Cor. 4:18

# THE END
## OF THE
# PILGRIMAGE

### Your Judgment Seat Verdict and How it Determines Your Place in His Kingdom

JAMES S. HOLLANDSWORTH

HOLLYPUBLISHING

# Dedication

To my wife Leslie,
my best friend for thirty years,
and faithful co-laborer in ministry.
We are in this together.

and ...

To the good people of Tri-City Baptist Church,
who have eagerly and graciously
received biblical teaching regarding
the Christ-life and persevering unto reward.
God bless you!

# Acknowledgements

I am truly grateful to my dear friends
who willingly reviewed this book before publication
and gave valuable input, both grammatical and theological.
Thank you for your wisdom and insight.
I am honored to have your friendship.

Matthew Barfield
Keith Call
Marty Cauley
Ernest Childs
Scott Crawford
Tracy Daniels
Joseph Dillow
Alan Robinson
Lewis & Charlotte Schoettle

All of these folks gave some degree of feedback,
and I appreciate their contribution.

Marty and Scott, through their excellent teaching on the
kingdom, have especially challenged me to consider that
rewards may be eternal (i.e., not merely lasting throughout
the millennium). See Marty's book, *Rewards Are Eternal*.

Lewis Schoettle, as you will learn from the Preface,
has impacted my life greatly for many years,
mainly through Schoettle Publishing Company.
I am thankful that he has kept the kingdom classics
in print for my generation.

I am also extremely grateful for Joseph Dillow's
massive tome, *Final Destiny*. His book,
more than any other, taught me what the Bible
says about persevering unto reward.

# Contents

Jesus will one day reclaim the kingdom that Adam forfeited to Satan. Christ will rule over the whole earth as King of Kings and Lord of Lords. He wants us to qualify to rule with Him. That is the purpose for which we have been created — to glorify God by co-ruling with Christ.

The aspect of salvation typically emphasized in the modern church is justification and positional sanctification of man's spirit. However, the Scriptures also stress the importance of soul-salvation for all saints, which is the ultimate goal of progressive sanctification.

Soul-salvation is costly. The price is denying self, taking up one's crosses and following Jesus. Only then, will one qualify to hear "well done" at the Judgment Seat and be qualified to rule with Jesus in the coming kingdom.

All children of God are unconditional heirs of God and therefore stand eternally secure. However, joint-heirship with Christ, which is the prerequisite for ruling with Him, is conditional, bestowed only upon those who qualify as firstborn sons by enduring their sufferings. Unfaithful, carnal saints could forfeit their conditional inheritance.

Jesus illustrated the principle of conditional inheritance by washing the disciples' feet. To have a part with Christ (i.e., fellowship with Him), we must be cleansed of sin that could hinder our fellowship with God. Saints are urged to make their "calling and election sure" by becoming partakers of Christ's nature and escaping the world's corruption, thereby assuring abundant entrance into the kingdom.

The popular understanding of Judgment Seat rewards is positive, but the Scriptures teach the prospect of negative rewards also. Jesus wants us to be faithful servants, ready for His return, not rebellious and unfaithful servants unprepared to meet Him. The consequences will be dire for those who are unprepared.

Will Jesus judge unconfessed sins at the Judgment Seat? Some say "absolutely not," on the basis that our sins are under the blood of Calvary. But what do the Scriptures teach? This chapter will focus on eight ways God judges sin in the life of the believer *now* and discusses the ramifications at the future Judgment Seat.

The kingdom of the heavens is the heavenly Jerusalem, the city of reward. It will be the headquarters for Christ's kingdom rule, and only qualified saints will dwell there in close proximity to Christ.

The righteous acts of faithful saints will become the white linen garment they will wear in the kingdom, signifying their holiness of life and status as a co-regent with Jesus. It is also the wedding garment, required for those who would be His bride and for inclusion at the wedding festivities. Unfaithful saints will not be granted white garments and will be excluded from the wedding. This is illustrated by the parable of the ten virgins.

Outer darkness is not a description of Hell, as commonly taught. It describes a realm of the kingdom — the negative counterpart to the positive city of reward. Those who are deemed unfaithful at the Judgment Seat will be in the outer darkness, a place of relative darkness on the outside of His bright ruling realm. Those saints consigned to the darkness outside will weep and gnash their teeth (consciously regret).

The Scriptures give several motivations for serving the Lord, including the prospect of positive reward. God has lovingly ordained it so. An entitlement, contractual mentality toward rewards is presumptuous and results in being last (least in the kingdom) rather than first (great in the kingdom).

Works-sanctification is a Satanic deception resulting in shame at the Judgment Seat. Works are not the *cause* of sanctification; they are the *effect*. Thus, God is pleased with sanctified (i.e., Spirit-enabled) works, not fleshly effort. Sanctification unto perfection happens over a lifetime. It is not the result of a spontaneous decision. The process of spiritual growth is outlined clearly in Rom. 5.

In the first of two chapters exploring the rewards for overcomers, a critical question will be answered: Are all Christians overcomers? The promise of eating of the tree of life will be examined as well as the enigma of not being hurt of the *second death*, which seems to be a reference to the lake of fire. How does this apply to saints?

Five additional rewards for overcomers are discussed, including the perplexing promise that the names of overcomers will not be blotted out of the book of life. Does this mean non-overcomers will be blotted out? Does this contradict the doctrine of eternal security?

Phil. 3:7-14 is a beautiful expression of the apostle Paul's longing to press toward the mark for the prize of the high calling and attain to the out-resurrection. His ambitions were "otherworldly." Ours should be too, if we would reign with Jesus.

# Preface

Seventeen years ago I met publisher Lewis Schoettle at a pastor's conference in Pennsylvania. Over the next several years we established a friendship, always meeting at the same conference. Little did I realize, at the time, the Lord was forging a long-term relationship that would impact my life.

Every year I would purchase stacks of Mr. Schoettle's used books, and he would try to convince me of the need to purchase some of the books he had published, largely reprints of nineteenth and early twentieth century authors, though I wasn't particularly interested in those. He was a good businessman, but I could sense he was not in it merely for the money. On the contrary, he was on a mission to teach me and other potential customers about the kingdom of God and the importance of preparing for it. With passion and candor, he would talk with me year after year, never seeming to get discouraged that I was not really warming up to his views. Nevertheless, he would always send me home with a couple of free books to whet my appetite.

I started reading those books and realized, very quickly, that the interpretive scheme employed for understanding the kingdom was very different from my own. I was intrigued, for the hermeneutic of these authors seemed to make sense of passages that had always troubled me. My kingdom pilgrimage had begun, alongside a recent discovery of the Christ-life, the key to victory and abundant life. In the Christ-life I had found the **provision** for progressive sanctification, and in my newfound discovery of kingdom truth I had found another **motivation** for preparing to meet Jesus at the Judgment Seat.

While my understanding of the Christ-life continued to grow during the first decade of the new millennium, unfortunately, my growth in kingdom truth was stunted, put on hold, by a foolish choice on my part. I had attended a local pastor's fellowship in those early years and put my neck on the line during a question and answer time amongst the men. I told the other pastors how I had recently become exposed to teaching about "millennial exclusion," and that I had come to realize that our verdict, as believers at the Judgment Seat, would determine whether or not we would inherit the millennial kingdom. I mentioned some of the nineteenth century authors to whom I had been exposed and asked if the men knew of any contemporary authors who had written on the subject, so I could read and study further.

My question invoked quite a reaction. Most of the men were completely perplexed, having never heard of that particular view or the authors, and did not know how to respond. Others sneered and chuckled, while one old timer bellowed out from the back of the room, "Just read your Bible, brother, and stay away from that heresy!" I was shocked and somewhat embarrassed by the ungracious handling of my sincere question. The conversation was over, and they were on to the next question.

The ugly response did not sway my convincement that what I was reading had a kernel of truth, but it did show me what I was up against. This was not mainstream dispensational eschatology, but why not? It would be many years before I could answer that question, for I am ashamed to admit I left the books (and that area of Scriptural study) on the shelf for more than a decade. While on a missions trip to India a few years ago, the Lord dealt with me about the account I must give at the Judgment Seat. I remembered the books and began a study that has not ended to this day.

I am truly grateful to the Holy Spirit for His guidance and help as I have studied the Word and this most important subject of the kingdom. My only regret is that I did not embrace these truths earlier in my life. Despite my failures, God's mercy is everlasting. I am also grateful to Mr. Lewis Schoettle for kindly staying after me. His faithfulness in publishing and sharing kingdom truth has impacted my life for the glory of the Lord. I trust he will be richly rewarded at the Bema.

James S. Hollandsworth
Forest City, North Carolina, 2015

# Chapter 1

---

# Two Kingdoms in Conflict

The Christian life is a pilgrimage. We are on a spiritual journey from one place to the next, from an earthly realm to a heavenly.

> These all died in faith, not having received the promises, but having seen them afar off, and were persuaded of them, and embraced them, and confessed that they were strangers and pilgrims on the earth. Heb. 11:13

> For our conversation (citizenship) is in heaven; from whence also we look for the Saviour, the Lord Jesus Christ: Phil. 3:20

> For we walk by faith, not by sight. 2 Cor. 5:7

The starting point of the pilgrimage is our salvation. The journey, ideally, is our progressive sanctification (being set apart) from sin and this present world unto righteousness and the world to come, otherwise known as the kingdom of Christ.

> Dearly beloved, I beseech you as strangers and pilgrims, abstain from fleshly lusts, which war against the soul. 1 Pet. 2:11

The end of our pilgrimage is the Judgment Seat of Christ, known in Greek as the *Bema*, the tribunal of Jesus. There He will judge every saint to determine whether we have been sanctified unto *perfection* (not sinlessness, but completion). The verdict could potentially be, *Well done, good and faithful servant*, or *Thou wicked and slothful servant*, (Matt. 25:23,26), depending on how we journey throughout life's pilgrimage. In other words, the reward could be positive or negative. Consequently, the verdict will determine our place in Christ's coming kingdom.

As we journey along in the Christian life, we discover very quickly that we are engaged in warfare. No child of God is exempt. The enemy is real and powerful and has many resources in his spiritual arsenal. Nevertheless, we have been given the necessary armor and weaponry for defeating him.

> For we wrestle not against flesh and blood, but against principalities, against powers, against the rulers of the darkness of this world, against spiritual wickedness in high places. Wherefore take unto you the whole armour of God. Eph. 6:12

> For though we walk in the flesh, we do not war after the flesh: (For the weapons of our warfare are not carnal, but mighty through God to the pulling down of strong holds;) 2 Cor. 10:3-4

We are all, by default, part of a cosmic conflict, whether we realize it or not. As citizens of Christ's future kingdom, we battle every day against the kingdom of Satan, from which we have been saved (Col. 1:13). Thankfully, we can be victorious, for our King defeated the enemy, through His death and resurrection (Heb. 2:14). The foe was rendered powerless, but his ultimate demise will come when our King returns to set up His kingdom. In the interim, while we wait, our Lord wants us to draw faithfully upon His power and authority — in other words, His provision — for spiritual victory. To that end, we must walk by faith, not by sight.

This volume is focused on the future consequences for victorious saints (i.e., *overcomers*) vs. defeated saints. The reader may be surprised to discover that only *overcomers* will rule with Jesus in His coming kingdom. What will happen to all the other saints? We will answer that question as we go along, and the answer may be shocking. In order to lay a proper foundation, we must start by taking a bird's-eye tour of the two kingdoms in conflict.

## The First Kingdom Forfeited

Adam was the first king of this world. His consort queen Eve ruled at his side. God gave them a realm, the entire earth. God intended for Adam initially, and all mankind subsequently, to rule over the entire created order, as God's representative on Earth. Man was to replenish (literally, fill up) the earth and subdue it and have dominion over every living thing. The three essential aspects of a kingdom were in place: a ruler, a realm, and actual rulership. Everything was perfect, just as God had intended.

> And God said, Let us make man in our image, after our likeness: and let them have dominion over the fish of the sea, and over the fowl of the air, and over the cattle, and over all the earth, and over every creeping thing that creepeth upon the earth. So God created man in his own image, in the image of God created he him; male and female created he them. And God blessed them, and God said unto them, Be fruitful, and multiply, and replenish the earth, and subdue it: and have dominion over the fish of the sea, and over the fowl of the air, and over every living thing that moveth upon the earth. And God saw every thing that he had made, and, behold, it was very good. Gen. 1:26-28, 31

If Adam had proceeded to follow God's perfect will, the entire human race would have continued ruling all of nature (Ps. 8:5-6). But God gave Adam a choice (Gen. 2:16-17; 3:6; Josh. 24:15). Despite his ideal surroundings (Gen. 2:8-15), Adam chose to sin and thereby forfeited his dominion over creation. Because of sin, the image of God in Adam was marred. His spirit became dead in trespasses and sins (Eph. 2:1), his soul became wicked and degenerate (Jer. 17:9; Ezek. 18:20), and his body became corrupted and eventually died (Rom. 6:23). The curse of sin affected the entire human race (Rom. 5:12) and separated man from God (Isa. 59:1-2).

Satan the tempter, who had provoked man's fall, consequently usurped man's authority. The kingdom became his (Luke 4:5-7; Matt. 12:26). It's not that God lost control of His kingdom because of Adam. On the contrary, God's kingdom is everlasting (Ps. 145:13; Dan. 4:3; 2 Pet. 1:11), and He is sovereign over all (Ps. 115:3; 103:19). But when man forfeited the earthly kingdom, God cursed man and the earth and Satan (Gen. 3:14-19), and allowed Satan to take control for a time until One would come to "crush the serpent's head" (Gen. 3:15).

## The Usurper Crushed

Thankfully, God had a plan to redeem lost mankind and to restore the theocracy. Indeed, in the fullness of time (Gal. 4:4) the Son of God left Heaven's glories; laid aside His divine prerogatives (Phil. 2:5-8); was born of a virgin (Isa. 7:14; Matt. 1:18-25); took on human flesh (Heb. 2:14; Phil. 2:5-8) — of the lineage of Abraham, Isaac, Jacob (Israel) and Judah — and lived a sinless life as the second Adam (1 Pet. 2:22; 2 Cor. 5:21; Heb. 4:15). He preached a message of repentance to His people (Matt. 4:17), but was rejected by them (John 1:11) and put to death, willingly enduring the horrors of crucifixion and shedding His precious blood on the cross of Calvary so that He might pay the price for sin as the perfect Lamb of God. Following His death and burial, the Messiah arose from the grave on the third day and thereby defeated sin and death and Satan. The serpent's head was crushed, rendering him powerless (Heb. 2:14). The devil is a defeated foe, even though he continues to rule temporarily. Jesus ascended into Heaven forty days after His resurrection, and He is now seated at the right hand of the Father, a place of exaltation (Eph. 1:19-20; Phil. 2:9-11). All powers have been placed under the feet of Jesus, including Satan's domain (Eph. 1:21-22a).

Those who receive His free gift of eternal life are reconciled with God (John 1:12), forgiven of all sin (past, present, future), and credited with the righteousness of Christ (2 Cor. 5:21). At salvation the spirit of man is made alive, passing from death unto life. Old things pass away; all things become new (2 Cor. 5:17). The Holy Spirit of God takes up permanent residence in regenerated saints. It is also accurate to say Christ lives within believers (Gal. 2:20). He becomes our provision when we, by faith, appropriate His grace (Rom. 5:2), letting Him live His life through us. To the extent the believer lives in this way, fully dependent on Christ, he will be abiding in the vine. Whoever abides in Him does not sin (1 John 3:6), as long as he continues abiding. Unfortunately, our problem is that we do not consistently abide in Christ.

Thus, the image of God is partly restored in man at the point of salvation, when his spirit is made alive. Throughout the Christian life, more of God's image is restored, to the extent the believer progresses in discipleship and his soul becomes sanctified by conformity to the image of Jesus. Those who submit to God's image-restoring plan in their lives (called progressive sanctification) enter into a kingdom way of living in this life, which then qualifies them to rule with Jesus in His coming kingdom.

## The Kingdom Restored

One day soon Jesus will gather up all of God's children into the heavenlies, those whom He has redeemed by His blood (1 Thess. 4:13-18). The saints will give an account of their lives at the Judgment Seat of Christ (2 Cor. 5:10). Following a seven-year period of tribulation on Earth (see Rev. 6-16), the primary purpose of which is to bring national Israel to repentance, Jesus will return to Earth, defeat the Gentile kingdoms of the world as controlled by Satan, and save the nation of Israel (Zech. 12:7, 10; Rom. 11:26). Then He will commence His Messianic kingdom on Earth, during which time Satan and his host will be bound and imprisoned in the bottomless pit (Rev. 20:1-3).

Christ will demonstrate that a kingdom of God on Earth — a kingdom from Heaven — is possible, as He rules in righteousness and peace for a thousand years. At the end of His millennial reign, Satan will be loosed to stir up a rebellion amongst men, but God will destroy them all from Heaven with fire, and will cast Satan into the lake of fire, along with death and hades (Rev. 20:7-10). Death will be no more (1 Cor. 15:25-26, 54-57; Rev. 21:4). The redeemed will live eternally in the new Heaven and/or new Earth (Rev. 21:1-5) and the condemned will suffer eternally in the lake of fire (Rev. 20:11-15; 21:8).

During the interim period between Christ's first coming and His second, Satan functions as the prince of this world (John 12:31; 14:30; 16:11), the prince of the power of the air who now works in the lives of unsaved men (Eph. 2:2; 2 Cor. 4:4). Along with his fallen echelon, he rules the world, both terrestrial and celestial by controlling the Gentile kingdoms of the world (Eph. 6:12). Notwithstanding, God intends to take back the kingdom through Jesus Christ, the second Adam. As demonstrated above, He has already won the victory and inherited the right to rule. Thus, Jesus is the rightful King, and He has been given a realm, His Church — those who have been translated from Satan's kingdom, the power of darkness, to the kingdom of Christ (Col. 1:13). Nevertheless, Jesus is not presently ruling as a King. Rather, He is presently functioning in His role as Priest, interceding for the saints (Rom. 8:27; Heb. 7:25-27). When He comes again, He will deal a death-blow to the enemies of God, take the kingdom from Satan, and become crowned as millennial king.

The purpose of the millennial kingdom is for Jesus, the second Adam, to rule in righteousness along with qualified, redeemed saints, and thereby demonstrate what could have happened under the first Adam, had he not sinned.

It is very important for children of God to recognize that our primary purpose for existence is to glorify God by living in a way that pleases Him now so that we can qualify to rule with Him then, over the world and over angels (1 Cor. 6:2-3). Co-ruling with Christ in His kingdom is the crown to which we aspire (Matt. 25:14-23). Not to win that prize is to fall short of our reason for living and will result in shame and regret (Matt. 25:24-30; 1 John 2:28).

## Knowing Therefore the Terror of the Lord ...

The kingdom was foremost in our Lord's earthly ministry. In His final forty days on Earth before ascending to Heaven, Jesus spoke to His disciples *of the things pertaining to the kingdom of God*, Acts 1:3. His future Messianic kingdom on Earth was the burden of His heart from the very start of His public ministry — *Repent: for the kingdom of heaven is at hand*, Matt. 4:17 — and it was on His heart to the very end.

Yet, His focus was not merely on the fact of the millennial kingdom or the nature of it. The Old Testament prophets had already said much concerning the coming Messianic kingdom.

Repeatedly, through the Synoptic Gospels, we find Jesus honing in on the requirements for living the kingdom way of life here and now, which then qualifies one to inherit the coming millennial kingdom.

If Jesus cared so much about getting His disciples ready for the kingdom, how much more should we? Is the church of Jesus Christ really focused on the kingdom? If so, then why are more Christians not being motivated to prepare for the Judgment Seat of Christ and what follows? Could it be that many do not take the Judgment Seat seriously?

The apostle Paul's warning should be sobering to us all:

> For we must all appear before the judgment seat of Christ; that every one may receive the things done in his body, according to that he hath done, whether it be good or bad. 2 Cor. 5:10

All children of God will appear (i.e., be made manifest) at the tribunal of Jesus. Every one will be recompensed according to how he lived on Earth. The verdict will be either good (*Well done, good and faithful servant*) or bad (*Thou wicked and slothful servant*) and will determine the extent of every man's reward or loss as he enters the Messianic kingdom of Christ on Earth.

> Every man's work shall be made manifest: for the day shall declare it, because it shall be revealed by fire; and the fire shall try every man's work of what sort it is. If any man's work abide which he hath built thereupon, he shall receive a reward. If any man's work shall be burned, he shall suffer loss: but he himself shall be saved; yet so as by fire. 1 Cor. 3:13-15

Work of an inferior nature (i.e., temporal and self-dependent) will be consumed in Christ's "testing" fire, and be considered a loss in the kingdom. That saint of God, though eternally secure, will be ashamed at the Judgment Seat, and will consciously regret his verdict throughout the millennial kingdom, having no opportunity to rule and reign with Christ (the very purpose of our millennial existence). Only work of an abiding nature (eternal and Christ-dependent) will survive and be rewarded in the kingdom.

Because we fear our God who is a consuming fire (Heb. 12:29), we should passionately convince fellow believers of their coming appointment.

> Knowing therefore the terror of the Lord, we persuade men. 2 Cor. 5:11

In other words, we should be actively engaged in warning saints of the awfulness of the Judgment Seat of Christ and helping them prepare to give a good account. This verse is most commonly used to emphasize the urgency of persuading lost folks to be saved from condemnation, and that is certainly a valid application. But the most immediate context (v. 10, quoted above) is persuading saved people to be ready to meet Jesus at the Judgment Seat.

Unfortunately, I believe an error has crept into the church in modern times. Many assume, because they are eternally secure, that the Judgment Seat of Christ will be merely an awards ceremony of sorts. They imagine shuddering momentarily at the Bema, perhaps receiving a mild rebuke, then continuing on into the millennial kingdom with all the honors and privileges supposedly conferred upon children of God. They expect a "happily-ever-after" millennial existence, with no tears or sorrow. Nothing could be further from the truth!

There are at least two problems with this mentality. First, it assumes all children of God are, by nature of their standing, automatically qualified to rule and reign as firstborn sons. But that is not what the Bible teaches, as we shall see. Second, it assumes the Judgment Seat of Christ will be a mere formality, no big deal. But this way of thinking is flippant and mis-informed and will certainly be regretted in the future.

Out of a passion to help saints prepare for the coming kingdom, I am offering this book to provide Biblical teaching on the coming Judgment Seat of Christ and the millennial kingdom of Jesus Christ to follow. Oh, may all saints of God prepare *now* to hear "well done" *then*, that they might glorify Christ by reigning together with Him in His coming kingdom.

# Chapter 2

---

# The Three Tenses of Salvation

Let's begin with a "pop" quiz, multiple choice. Which answer best describes your relationship with the Lord?

a. I have been saved.
b. I will be saved.
c. I am being saved.
d. all of the above.

Of course, the correct answer for all born-again children of God is "d. all of the above."

## I have been saved

In one word, this is the doctrine of **justification**. At the point of salvation, you were justified and regenerated, redeemed by the blood of Christ. Therefore, you have been saved. You have been declared righteous by God, and your sins have been forgiven, and your account has been credited with the righteousness of Christ. You have been given an entirely new nature. You have been sanctified positionally. All of that happened in the past tense. It has already occurred, as in a legal transaction. Yet it is much more than a mere transaction. It is a reality, for Christ now lives in you by His Holy Spirit!

> And such were some of you: but ye are (have been) washed, but ye are (have been) sanctified, but ye are (have been) justified in the name of the Lord Jesus, and by the Spirit of our God. 1 Cor. 6:11

> Therefore, if any man be in Christ he is a new creature: old things are passed away; behold, all things are become new. 2 Cor. 5:17

> And you hath he quickened, who were dead in trespasses and sins; Eph. 2:1

> Ye (have) put on the new man, which after God is created in righteousness and true holiness. Eph. 4:24

> Ye have put off the old man with his deeds; And have put on the new man, which is renewed in knowledge after the image of him that created him: Col. 3:9-10

Moreover, Scripture seems to indicate this past-tense transaction of salvation took place within the realm of your human spirit, which is distinct from the soul. Some take the position that man is dichotomous, or two parts — physical and metaphysical or material and immaterial. However, the Bible teaches that man is trichotomous, or three parts, comprised of spirit, soul, and body. Consider the following passages:

> And the very God of peace sanctify you wholly; and I pray God your whole spirit and soul and body be preserved blameless unto the coming of our Lord Jesus Christ. 1 Thess. 5:23

> For the word of God is quick, and powerful, and sharper than any two-edged sword, piercing even to the dividing asunder of soul and spirit, and of the joints and marrow, and is a discerner of the thoughts and intents of the heart. Heb. 4:12

While man cannot divide between soul and spirit, God can. In fact, Heb. 4:12 seems to emphasize that God — through His Word — wants man to learn the distinction between soul and spirit. Why is this so important? Because the Bible teaches there are two (metaphysical) salvations, or we could say two key aspects of salvation — the salvation of the spirit as something distinct from the salvation of the soul.

The spirit of man is reserved for God-consciousness, and prior to salvation is dead in trespasses and sins. It is made alive at regeneration.

> That which is born of the flesh is flesh; and that which is born of the Spirit is spirit. John 3:6

> If Christ be in you, the body is dead because of sin; but the spirit is life because of righteousness. Rom. 8:10

> The Spirit itself beareth witness with our spirit, that we are the children of God: Rom. 8:16

Scripture is abundantly clear that salvation has a "past tense" component. You *have been* saved — justified — and that work of God took place in your spirit.

## I will be saved

Moving from the past to the future, you *will be* saved when you meet Jesus face to face. That will happen when your body is reunited with soul and spirit at the rapture or some time shortly thereafter (perhaps at the Bema). The doctrinal term for this aspect of salvation is **redemption** — when the earthly body of corruption will be given a resurrected body, equipped for existence in the eternal state.

> Even we ourselves groan within ourselves, waiting for the adoption, to wit, the redemption of our body. Rom. 8:23

> After that ye believed, ye were sealed with that holy Spirit of promise, which is the earnest of our inheritance until the redemption of the purchased possession, Eph. 1:13-14

> Grieve not the holy Spirit of God, whereby ye are sealed unto the day of redemption. Eph. 4:30

Some like to use the doctrinal term *glorification* when speaking of future salvation, and glorification is certainly future. However, I prefer to use the term *redemption*, because in my opinion, while the bodies of all saints will be redeemed (as indicated in the above verses), they will not all be glorified. Glorification is a concept of exaltation that, in the eternal state, seems to be accompanied by a glow in some degree (e.g., Christ's body on the Mount of Transfiguration, Matt. 17:1-9). Unfaithful saints apparently will not have that glow, for it is reserved for those who have suffered with Christ and have remained faithful and, therefore, will glow with Him in the eternal state (Rom. 8:17; 29-30). Exaltation seems out of character for unfaithful saints. We will touch on this subject again in Chapter 14.

Technically speaking, the realm of the body is not yet saved. Is that not obvious? The body declines throughout its earthly existence until it eventually dies and decays in the ground. Paul called it, *the body of this death*, Rom. 7:24. Nevertheless, the bodies of believers will be saved one day!

You *have been* saved. At some point in your past, God justified, regenerated, and sanctified you positionally. It happened in your spirit, which the Holy Spirit made alive. In the future you *will be* saved, when Jesus reunites your soul and spirit with a resurrected body. What about the present?

## I am being saved.

You *are being* saved. This aspect of salvation is known as **sanctification**, particularly the progressive or experiential aspect of sanctification, becoming more like Christ. Experiential sanctification happens in the realm of the soul, which is comprised of mind (intellect), emotions (feelings), and will (volition). You have all the provision necessary (Gal. 2:20) for progressing in the sanctification of your soul, because your spirit has already been sanctified positionally.

However, spiritual progression is not automatic. You must choose to appropriate the provision. Daily, moment-by-moment choices must be made to depend upon the enabling power of the Holy Spirit within your spirit to lead your soul and then for your soul to lead the body, *in that order* (see diagram on p. 28). When a believer reverses the order, allowing the bodily desires or soulish passions to rule, carnality results, and the Spirit of God is grieved. Carnality may be temporary or could potentially continue indefinitely.

The salvation of the soul is to be distinguished from the salvation of the spirit. Thus, it is correct theologically to say the Bible speaks of two (metaphysical) salvations, not merely one. Of course, we understand that the soul cannot be saved (progressively sanctified) unless the spirit is first saved. As already demonstrated, the salvation of the spirit is a thing of the past and impacts eternal destiny, whereas the salvation of the soul is a thing of the present and impacts eternal rewards (positive or negative).

> Wherefore lay apart all filthiness and superfluity of naughtiness, and receive with meekness the engrafted word, which is able to save your souls. James 1:21

> Receiving the end of your faith, even the salvation of your souls. 1 Pet. 1:9

> But we are not of them who draw back unto perdition; but of them that believe to the saving of the soul. Heb. 10:39

> Dearly beloved, I beseech you as strangers and pilgrims, abstain from fleshly lusts, which war against the soul. 1 Pet. 2:11

Following is a summary of the three tenses of salvation.

| THE THREE TENSES OF SALVATION | | |
|---|---|---|
| PAST | PRESENT | FUTURE |
| I have been saved | I am being saved | I will be saved |
| Justification | Sanctification | Redemption |
| Spirit | Soul | Body |

Does this mean that only one-third of a believer is actually saved? It depends on how one defines the word *saved*. From man's perspective, the whole man is saved, because we are incapable of separating spirit, soul and body. However, God is able to divide asunder the three parts of man, and so theologically, it is accurate to refer to them independently. We have a responsibility to recognize what God has done, what He is doing, and what He will do in each part of our being!

## The Battle for the Soul

A battle rages for the soul. It is the part of you that is being saved (or not) in the present, and it is the aspect of your being that will be judged at the Bema. Satan wants to keep your soul from being saved, but Jesus wants you to be an experiential overcomer. Indeed, He died so you can have victory.

Incidentally, the battle is not between the new nature (a redeemed spirit) and a so-called old nature, as if they were level playing fields. The Bible makes clear, *Old things are passed away; behold, all things are become new,* 2 Cor. 5:17.

The battle is between a righteous spirit and a sinful soul that lives in an unredeemed body. The latter two are partners in crime, the two working together, soul and body collectively referred to as the *flesh.* This prompted Paul to cry out in Rom. 7:24, *O wretched man that I am! who shall deliver me from the body of this death?*

The apostle's sinful soul was working in league with his unredeemed body, holding him back from serving God. He refers to it as the law of sin and death (Rom. 8:2) or indwelling sin. But in the same verse Paul reveals the secret of victory over this law. It is another law, the law of the spirit of life in Christ that frees believers from the law of sin and death. Some call it the law of counteraction. It is like a hot air balloon pilot overcoming the law of gravity by heating the air inside the balloon. If he refuses to believe the hot air will lift the balloon, he will never apply the heat. So it is with a child of God who does not appropriate the enabling power of the Holy Spirit to live the Christ life.

The sinfulness of your soul can be overcome by the righteous One who lives within your spirit (which has been made righteous). In the spirit realm of your being the seed of God (Greek, *sperma*) remains, and you cannot sin (1 John 3:9). Therefore, your soul is being saved to the extent you are letting the law of the Spirit of life counteract the law of sin and death in your members. **The degree of your reward (positive or negative) at the Judgment Seat will be determined by the extent to which your soul is saved in this life.**

It is critically important to understand the difference between the two metaphysical salvations.

| SALVATION OF THE SPIRIT | SALVATION OF THE SOUL |
|---|---|
| What lost people need | What saved people need |
| Good News about eternal life (also bad news about sin & eternal condemnation) | Good news about inheritance (also bad news about disobedience & disinheritance) |
| Jesus as Savior | Jesus as Lord and King |
| Point-in-time decision | Lifetime process |
| Results in justification and eternal security | Results in sanctification and inheritance |
| A gift based on faith | A reward based on Spirit-enabled works |
| Unconditional - heirs of God | Conditional - co-heirs with Christ |
| No judgment | Judgment Seat |

Many students of the Scriptures fail to differentiate between the two salvations and thereby commit a serious hermeneutical (interpretative) error. For instance, passages that refer to the saving of the soul, intended for Christians, are frequently applied to the lost and their need to get saved. Passages about the possibility of losing the soul are equated with going to Hell. Passages about the kingdom of heaven or kingdom of God are relegated to Heaven, not the coming kingdom of our Lord Jesus Christ.

These are all dreadful mistakes and result in misinterpreting the book of Hebrews and passages in James and Matthew and, for that matter, much of the New Testament. It is a tragedy, for the church of Jesus Christ has not been taught to prepare for the Judgment Seat and the kingdom to follow.

For Christians to be prepared to give a good account at the Judgment Seat they must go all the way with Christ in discipleship so that He deems their soul to be saved and worthy of reward. Contrary to popular opinion, the soul is not automatically saved when the spirit is saved. Soul-salvation is a lifelong process, and Jesus does not instantaneously declare all saints perfectly sanctified at the Judgment Seat. He announces a verdict for each one, whether positive or negative. The verdict determines how they live out their kingdom existence, as we shall see in later chapters.

While eternal salvation is determined at a past point in time, it is only the beginning. The work of salvation in its complete sense (from God's perspective) continues over one's lifetime. Though we often refer to the ongoing aspect as *progressive sanctification*, it is technically part of God's complete salvation "package," and is accurately described as salvation of the soul. How one fares regarding the saving of his soul will be determined at the Judgment Seat.

Salvation of the spirit is a gift from God (John 3:16; Eph. 2:8-9) that anyone can receive now, by faith alone in the finished work of Christ; whereas salvation of the soul is a reward from Jesus, based on the quality of one's work for Him, that only believers will receive in the future … or not.

# Chapter 3

# The Paradox of Saving the Soul

Scripture is abundantly clear that salvation of the soul is not automatic. Every believer must choose to cooperate with God in the process. Those who do not make choices in accordance with the will of God will lose their soul. Notice the words of Christ:

> 24 Then said Jesus unto his disciples, If any man will come after me, let him deny himself, and take up his cross, and follow me.
> 25 For whosoever will save his life shall lose it: and whosoever will lose his life for my sake shall find it.
> 26 For what is a man profited, if he shall gain the whole world, and lose his own soul? or what shall a man give in exchange for his soul?
> 27 For the Son of man shall come in the glory of his Father with his angels; and then he shall reward every man according to his works.
> 28 Verily I say unto you, There be some standing here, which shall not taste of death, till they see the Son of man coming in his kingdom. Matt. 16:24-28

This passage is not a warning for unbelievers. If it were, then Jesus would be preaching salvation by works. On the contrary, Jesus is speaking to His disciples. By extension that includes us. He challenges us to live for the eternal rather than for the here and now. If we choose to *save* (i.e., preserve) our soul now — in other words, live to please ourselves — we will *lose* our soul at the Judgment Seat. It will not be saved, in the sense of being sanctified. All will be lost, consumed, in God's testing furnace. *The fire shall try every man's work of what sort it is*, 1 Cor. 3:13. On the other hand, if we choose to *lose* our soul now — that is, die to self — then our soul will be saved, preserved at the Bema, and rewarded by Christ. Notice the two paradoxes in Christ's teaching.

## Paradox #1: Save Now; Lose Later

Jesus warned of the possibility of an eternally-secure believer losing his soul at the Judgment Seat of Christ. This does not mean he will be denied eternal life, for his spirit has been justified and regenerated. Rather, losing one's soul at the Judgment Seat is the equivalent of what the apostle Paul described in 1 Cor. 3:15, *saved, yet so as by fire*. It is the prospect of suffering loss, shamefully entering the kingdom with no reward, and no glory. The very thought should make us shudder.

### Losing One's Soul

The King James translators interchanged the words *life* (v. 25) and *soul* (v. 26) in this passage, though they are translations of the same Greek word, *psuche* (or *psyche*), which means *soul*. Thus, verse 25 could be read, *For whosoever will save his **soul** shall lose it: and whosoever will lose his **soul** for my sake shall find it.*

What does it mean to lose one's soul and to save one's soul? Some have mistakenly concluded that to *lose* one's soul means to be eternally condemned — to *perish*, as the word is translated in John 3:16 and other places in the New Testament. How do we know to *lose* one's soul here in Matt. 16 does not refer to eternal condemnation? There are four indications in the text.

First, this particular Greek word is also translated *lose* and *lost* several times in the New Testament, but does not mean to perish or to be eternally condemned. For example, Luke 15 gives the parable of the man who has one hundred sheep but *loses* one of them. The man certainly does not perish, nor does his sheep. Rather, he is deprived of his possession, and that is how the word is used in Matt. 16. One who does not deprive self of his soul's desires here and now, will be deprived of his soul's desires in the age to come. In that sense his soul will be lost. On the other hand, one who deprives himself now — by denying self and taking up his cross — his soul will not be lost (deprived or forfeited), but found (rewarded)!

Second, Jesus is speaking with His disciples here, and in all the parallel passages (Matt. 10:39; Mark 8:35; Luke 9:24; 17:33; John 12:25), about the costs of discipleship. These are already saved men. They don't need to know how to be saved. They need to know how to *come after* Jesus and *follow* Him. Incidentally, following Jesus is a process, not a point-in-time event like justification. Clearly, this passage has nothing to do with the new birth. Jesus is teaching here about ongoing sanctification.

Third, if the means of salvation from eternal condemnation is denying self and taking up one's cross, then salvation would be by works, not of faith alone. However, salvation is by faith alone. Denying self and taking up one's cross is only possible when a believer depends upon the indwelling Spirit to enable to take such radical behavioral steps. An unbeliever is dead in trespasses and sins and therefore unable to obey God.

Fourth, verse 27 ties soul-salvation to the time when Jesus will *reward every man according to his works*. Some say that is a reference to the Great White Throne Judgment when the dead are judged *according to their works,* Rev. 20:12. However, Jesus gives a clear indication in vs. 27-28 as to which judgment is in question. The Son of Man coming *in the glory of his Father* (v. 27) is equated with the Son of man coming *in his kingdom* (v. 28), which is an obvious reference to the millennial kingdom that is preceded by the Bema, a judgment for believers only. Adding further credence to this view is Jesus' prediction that some standing there (whom we know to be Peter, James, and John) would not die until they would see Jesus coming in His kingdom. Contextually, this is a reference to the transfiguration, which is fulfilled just six days later (Matt. 17:1-9). Jesus gives His inner circle a glimpse of His glorified, kingdom body.

In summary, losing one's soul has nothing to do with eternal condemnation. It is being deprived of it at the Judgment Seat. It is suffering loss (1 Cor. 3:15) rather than receiving rewards. It is entering the millennial kingdom without glory, not being able to enjoy the incredible wonders of the age to come, and consciously regretting that more spiritual choices were not made in this life.

The paradox of Christ's teaching is that a believer loses his soul at the Judgment Seat by *saving* it here and now, in this life; that is, by refusing to deny self, take up his cross, and follow Jesus. Instead, he caters to self, avoids hardships and pays lip service to following Jesus, not counting the cost of discipleship.

In Luke 17 Jesus precedes His discussion of saving/losing one's soul with an admonition: *Remember Lot's wife,* Luke 17:32. It is important to remember that this Old Testament woman was righteous (justified), as her husband Lot, and because of her righteous standing before God, she was also delivered from Sodom. But despite the warnings of the angels, she turned and looked back, and instantly became a pillar of salt. She gained the world (*saved* her soul), and thereby forfeited her soul. Lot's wife is a metaphor for saints who *lose* their soul by *saving* it.

What a tragedy it would be for God's children to live for themselves now, in this fleeting, vapor-like life, only to discover at the future Judgment Seat of Christ that they had forfeited many eternal blessings God had intended for them.

Would it be worth it? Jesus warned on several occasions of the consequences (Matt. 10:39; 16:25; Mark 8:35; Luke 9:24; 17:33; John 12:25). Now let's look at the other side of the paradox:

## Paradox #2: Lose Now; Save Later

Those who *lose* now will *save* later. What does this mean? In v. 24 Jesus puts out the call for His children to *come after me* and *follow me*. That is the essence of discipleship. Of course, there is a price to pay, here and now, but there are serious eternal consequences for those who do not heed His call.

*Coming after* and *following* imply continuation, an ongoing process. This obviously cannot refer to the initial salvation of one's spirit, that is, justification, regeneration and positional sanctification. Those wonderful theological truths occurred at a point in time in the past, like a transaction, for those who have been born again. They are not processes.

Rather, *coming after* and *following* are the expected *results* of initial salvation, the realm of practical or experiential sanctification, which is the aspect of salvation that continues (*I am being saved.*) until we meet Christ at the Bema. Nevertheless, following Jesus is not automatic. God will never force His children to progress in sanctification. He may bring pressures to bear (i.e., discipline, Heb. 12), but ultimately God has left us with the choice to follow or not. As He does His part (Phil. 2:13), we must choose to do our part (Phil. 2:12), by ongoing decisions of faith, to cooperate with Him. Thus, Jesus warns of the consequences of not following, while clearly defining the costs and the benefits (rewards) of following. In other words, our Lord is encouraging His children to do a cost-benefit analysis and determine that it is worth it! Not to mention, as the apostle Paul points out, it is our *reasonable service*, Rom. 12:1.

## The Costs of Discipleship

What are the costs of discipleship? Not surprisingly, they all involve restraining the passions of the soul. Because of indwelling sin (Rom. 7:17, 20), the soul must be checked to keep it from ruling the spirit of man. If left to itself, the soul will trump the spirit and lead the whole man. The result is carnality in the life of a believer. God's will is that the spirit of man, where the Holy Spirit resides, be in the lead — spirit directing soul and soul directing body, *in that order*. See the diagram on p. 28.

## Denying Self

To truly follow Jesus one must deny self. That involves setting aside personal preferences and ambitions, and renouncing rights. This qualification for discipleship goes against the grain of our natural desires and passions. Even after becoming regenerated, self is very much alive and well, desiring to be catered unto. But self must be subjected in order for Jesus to be Lord of one's life.

The Holy Spirit always produces balance in the life of a believer by helping him to divide rightly and apply the Word of God. He will lead away from indulgence, on the one hand, and from asceticism, on the other. His way is moderation and temperance, control of self, as one depends on the Spirit for enablement.

The problem for most Christians is typically indulgence — loving the world — the lusts of the flesh, the lusts of the eyes, the pride of life. These will all pass away, but the one who does the will of God will abide forever. Constantly abiding in the vine is the opposite of routinely indulging in the world. Do you love shopping? Eating? Clothing? Possessions? Personal pampering and comforts? Sensuality? Entertainment? Relationships? Technology? Fill in the blank with whatever your flesh loves and craves. It has to go in order for the soul to be saved.

Another realm to be renounced is a high and lofty opinion of one's self, typically at the expense of others. Oftentimes, self manifests in the form of contentions (in its many varieties) — sarcasm, insults, verbal exchanges, derogatory speech, clamor, slander, physical fighting, etc. The source of all contention is pride and selfishness.

Only by pride cometh contention. Prov. 13:10

From whence come wars and fightings among you? come they not hence, even of your lusts that war in your members? James 4:1

But if ye have bitter envying and strife in your hearts, glory not, and lie not against the truth. This wisdom descendeth not from above, but is earthly, sensual, devilish. James 3:14-15

Wouldn't it be a tragedy to forfeit rewards at the Judgment Seat because self could not be conquered? The beauty of salvation is that we have been made righteous already and sanctified positionally in our spirit by the Holy Spirit. He lives within, providing everything necessary for us to be participants in His divine nature and thereby escape the world's corruptions through lust (2 Pet. 1:4). Our positional sanctification can be experienced — and indeed, must be! — in our everyday soul life, to the extent that we depend on the Spirit to live the Christ life.

The first cost of discipleship, denying self, demands a high price. The stakes are raised even higher in the second cost of discipleship, which is found in v. 24.

## Taking Up One's Cross

A cross is an instrument of torture and death. Jesus willingly took up His. He chose to leave Heaven's glories, lay aside His divine prerogatives, and take on human flesh. He chose to endure the horrors of crucifixion, knowing it was the will of the Father.

> I lay down my life ... No man taketh it from me, but I lay it down of myself. I have power to lay it down, and I have power to take it again. John 10:18

> My meat is to do the will of him that sent me, and to finish his work. John 4:34

He wants us to be willing to take up whatever He has taken up for us in the way of suffering and perhaps even death. The apostle Paul prayed,

> That I may know him, and the power of his resurrection, and the fellowship of his sufferings, being made conformable unto his death. Phil. 3:10

That is a heart that desires to take up its cross. In Luke 9:23 Jesus specified that our cross needs to be taken up *daily*.

However, it is important to clarify that a "cross" is not something you bring upon yourself — suffering as the consequence of sin or as the result of making foolish decisions. A "cross" is some form of suffering that God brings along your path. It could be a major financial reversal or a serious health condition or some form of persecution. Whatever cross God allows in your life, you must choose to take it up, which means to respond rightly to the crisis. Count it all joy when you face various kinds of trials (James 1:2). God promises His grace *is* sufficient to endure the trial (2 Cor. 12:9). Your responsibility is to take up the cross, not chafe at it or lean to your own understanding and try to sidestep it. Notice that "taking up" requires a decision of your will to embrace the cross, which is God's will. Again, this is referring to the realm of the soul. It does not come natural to us. We must choose to take it up.

Are you actively seeking by the power of the Holy Spirit to lose your soul now? It means letting go of that which your soul craves, the pleasures of life, the high opinion of self. It means choosing to suffer willingly for Jesus, rejoicing in your crosses. If you will deny self and take up your cross in order to follow Him, your soul will be lost now (with respect to the world), but gained at the Judgment Seat. You will receive the true object of your heart's affection: Jesus in all His glory.

To lose one's soul now is far better than losing it at the Judgment Seat. Those who lose their soul at the Judgment Seat will surely regret it. Better to lose now and save later.

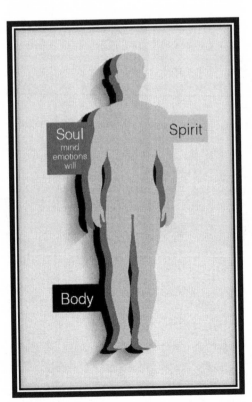

## A Rightly Ordered Life

*Man is comprised of spirit, soul, and body. When the Holy Spirit fills a Christian, that believer's spirit leads his soul in righteousness. The body follows along. This is a rightly ordered life in which the soul is being saved. However, a believer that is not Spirit-filled will submit to fleshly appetites, putting the body or soul in the lead, which is out of God's order.*

# Chapter 4

# No Guarantees

For years I misread an oft-quoted verse of Scripture.

> The Spirit itself beareth witness with our spirit, that we are the children of God: And if children, then heirs; heirs of God, and joint-heirs with Christ; if so be that we suffer with him, that we may be also glorified together. Rom. 8:16-17

In my defense, I never heard this passage preached or taught correctly, that I can remember. But, to my shame, I fell into a trap — and the trap is making assumptions about Scripture passages rather than honestly interpreting the passages, even if the interpretation doesn't fit our theological grid.

I personally believe that is a major problem in Bible-believing Christianity — assuming, based on what we have been taught. But what if our teachers were incorrect on a particular point? Are we obligated to perpetuate an erroneous tradition? God forbid! I appreciate my teachers, and learned much from them, but I am now convinced they missed some things, and I'm sure I have too – not one of us has all the answers. That is why having a teachable spirit is so critical. Putting aside preconceived notions, let's approach this Scripture passage with an open mind.

I always assumed all believers become both heirs of God and joint-heirs with Christ at the point of salvation, as if there were a period at the end of that statement. However, I have since realized that, according to the verse, inheritance with Christ is conditional – *if so be that we suffer with him*. Somehow, I had missed that.

## Two Inheritances

In the Bible, we find not **one** inheritance for Christians, but **two**. The first is an unconditional inheritance. It is guaranteed and bestowed on all saints based on our *position* in Christ. The inheritance is the gift of eternal life, because we are sons of God and, as sons, heirs of God.

> Wherefore thou art no more a servant, but a son; and if a son, then an heir of God through Christ. Gal. 4:7

The other inheritance is conditional. It is not guaranteed, but is awarded at the Judgment Seat only to those who qualify, based on obedience and faithfulness in stewardship (i.e., soul-salvation — how one progresses in sanctification). The inheritance is the privilege of ruling in the coming kingdom as Christ's co-heir. Notice the following chart:

| Unconditional Inheritance | Conditional Inheritance |
|---|---|
| Guaranteed | Not guaranteed |
| Gift of eternal life | Rewards for service |
| Bestowed on all saints | Awarded to qualified saints |
| Based on position in Christ - "heirs of God" | Based on faithfulness - "co-heirs with Christ" |
| Present in the kingdom | Ruling in the kingdom |

Our unconditional inheritance can never be forfeited, for it is based on sonship, and all believers are sons of God. However, our conditional inheritance can be forfeited, for it is based on qualifying as a firstborn son.

In Bible times, firstborn sons received a double portion. That is, they received not only the regular portion bestowed upon all sons, but also an additional portion. Nevertheless, while it was referred to commonly as the inheritance of the firstborn, the father was under no obligation to give it to the firstborn. He could choose to give it to another, if he did not deem the firstborn son worthy of the firstborn inheritance. In other words, if a firstborn son disqualified himself for some reason, he would lose the special inheritance for firstborn sons.

A classic example of this is Jacob and sons. Reuben was the firstborn son and normally would have received the double inheritance, but Reuben disqualified himself by taking his father's concubine as his own. Thus, Jacob pronounced Reuben unworthy of receiving the double inheritance and, instead, gave it to Joseph, blessing Joseph's two sons, Ephraim and Manasseh. Reuben still received the unconditional inheritance guaranteed to all sons, but he did not receive the conditional firstborn inheritance. That was given to another who was declared worthy.

## Israel's Example

God reminds New Testament Christians, *All these things happened unto them* (Old Testament Israel) *for ensamples: and they are written for our admonition, upon whom the ends of the world are come,* 1 Cor. 10:11. In other words, what happened to Old Testament Israel is to serve as a spiritual example to us, so that we might learn and not repeat the mistakes of Israel.

Consider the Exodus (Exod. 12:21-28). How many of the Israelites — at the point of the Exodus, when they left Egypt — were saved people? Every one of them! How do we know this? They *all* believed God, and they *all* applied the blood to the doorposts, as God had said. The angel of death passed over *all* of them, and they were *all* delivered from bondage in Egypt. Of course, the Passover is a beautiful picture of salvation in Jesus Christ, *the Lamb of God, which taketh away the sin of the world,* John 1:29. Thus, we sing that wonderful hymn, "When I see the blood, I will pass, I will pass over you."

Knowing the entire nation of Israel was saved at the Exodus, what does God have to say about their inheritance? First, they received an unconditional, guaranteed inheritance. Jehovah God declared Himself to be the God of Israel. Their inheritance was Jehovah.

> And I will dwell among the children of Israel, and will be their God. And they shall know that I am the Lord their God, that brought them forth out of the land of Egypt, that I may dwell among them: I am the Lord their God. Exod. 29:45-46

God said this long before Israel took possession of Canaan land. His unconditional promise (their unconditional inheritance) was that He would be their God. Obviously, those born after the Exodus would have to decide whether to believe on Jehovah and thereby enter into the national promise. In like manner, individuals today need to make their own decision to depend on Christ alone for salvation and thereby enter into the unconditional inheritance of the gift of eternal life that He bestows upon all who believe.

What was their conditional inheritance? While the land belonged unconditionally to the nation, according to the Abrahamic covenant (Gen. 17:7-8), it could be possessed only by those who believed God for victory over the enemy.

> Now therefore hearken, O Israel, unto the statutes and unto the judgments, which I teach you, for to do them, that ye may live, and go in and possess the land which the Lord God of your fathers giveth you. Deut. 4:1

> And thou shalt do that which is right and good in the sight of the Lord: that it may be well with thee, and that thou mayest go in and possess the good land which the Lord sware unto thy fathers. Deut. 6:18

> For if ye shall diligently keep all these commandments which I command you, to do them, to love the Lord your God, to walk in all his ways, and to cleave unto him; Then will the Lord drive out all these nations from before you, and ... every place whereon the soles of your feet shall tread shall be yours. Deut. 11:22-24

The condition for inheriting (i.e., taking possession of) the land was obedience to God's Word and faithfulness (i.e., full dependence on the Lord for victory). Here's the point: saved

Israelites unconditionally received God as their inheritance, but possession of Canaan land was conditional, depending on their obedience and faithfulness to Jehovah.

Some make the mistake of equating Canaan land with Heaven, but that is an error of interpretation (a hermeneutical error). Canaan land is a picture of two things: 1) spiritual victory in the present life, which leads to 2) inheriting promised rest (i.e., the reward of rest) in the age to come. Incidentally, even after taking possession of Canaan land the Israelites had the potential of losing it, if they were to become unfaithful — see Deut. 28:58, 63.

## Millennial Inheritance — the Reward for Faithfulness

As children of God, we are guaranteed eternal life; we already have this aspect of inheritance as heirs of God. However, we are not guaranteed millennial inheritance; that is the reward for faithfulness. All believers will be in some realm of the millennial world, but not all will inherit that kingdom or enjoy the benefits of ruling and reigning with Christ.

I liken that condition to being a subject in a medieval kingdom, for example. The king would own and rule a vast territory. His subjects would benefit from living in the village, under the king's protection and bounty, but only those heirs living in the castle would be able to fully participate in reigning and enjoy the beauties and luxuries and opportunities of the king Himself.

There is a difference between merely living in the kingdom and inheriting it, just as there was a difference for Israel living in the Promised Land and taking possession of it (see Deut. 11:31). Abraham sojourned in Canaan land, but He did not possess it, according to Heb. 11:9, 13. Furthermore, for many centuries of Israel's existence in the land, they did not possess the land, even though they lived there. Instead, foreign powers controlled the land and taxed the Israelites.

Possession of the Promised Land was God's intent for Israel from the very beginning of the nation's salvation. Indeed, God introduced Israel to Pharaoh as His firstborn son (conditional inheritance).

And thou shalt say unto Pharaoh, Thus saith the Lord, Israel is my son, even my firstborn: Exod. 4:22

Nevertheless, for those Israelites (twenty years old and above) who did not believe God for taking the Promised Land but rather tested God in the wilderness, ultimately at Kadesh-Barnea, they were disinherited from entering the Promised Land, because they disqualified themselves. Even Moses was denied entrance because of disobedience!

It was only after Joshua and Caleb led the people to believe God for victory to conquer Canaan land that they were able to enter. But even later, after Israel was dwelling in the land, the nation forfeited its conditional inheritance through disobedience, and so God removed them from the land.

And so with Christians, from the very day of your salvation, God's desire is to give you kingdom inheritance. Incidentally, for those whom God knows will cooperate with Him in the sanctification process, He predestines them to the status of firstborn sons, inheritors!

For whom he did foreknow, he also did predestinate to be conformed to the image of his Son, that he might be the firstborn among many brethren. Rom. 8:29

God predestines those whom He knows will be faithful, to conformity to Christ (i.e., Christ living His life through theirs), which qualifies them to remain in the status of firstborn sons, as Jesus. He wants to be the firstborn among many brethren. But many disinherit themselves from that blessing by lifestyle choices, by living unto themselves, unfaithfully, in disobedience (i.e., not in dependence on Christ for sanctification).

## The Danger of Disinheritance

The apostle Paul warns repeatedly of the danger of disinheritance.

We are bound to thank God always for you, brethren, as it is meet, because that your faith groweth exceedingly, and the charity of every one of you all toward each other aboundeth; So that we ourselves glory in you in the churches of God for your patience and faith in all your persecutions and tribulations that ye endure:

Which is a manifest token of the righteous judgment of God, that ye may be counted worthy of the kingdom of God, for which ye also suffer. 2 Thess. 1:3-5

How can one be *counted worthy* of the kingdom of God? Is Paul teaching works-salvation? Of course not! Paul is not speaking about matters of salvation, or we could say, unconditional inheritance. He is speaking to saints about sanctification, that is, conditional inheritance.

Of course, he is referring to the Judgment Seat. That is the place where one will ultimately be found worthy or unworthy of inheriting the kingdom. On that day, the works of all who are in Christ will be tried by fire, to determine *what sort it is*, 1 Cor. 3:13. If one's work abides (being of the gold-silver-precious stones type), a reward will be given. On the contrary, if one's work is burned (being of the wood-hay-stubble type), all will be lost, yet the individual will be saved eternally. What is it that can be lost or forfeited at the Judgment Seat?

Know ye not that the unrighteous shall not inherit the kingdom of God? Be not deceived: neither fornicators, nor idolaters, nor adulterers, nor effeminate, nor abusers of themselves with mankind, nor thieves, nor covetous, nor drunkards, nor revilers, nor extortioners, shall inherit the kingdom of God. 1 Cor. 6:9-10

Now the works of the flesh are manifest, which are these; Adultery, fornication, uncleanness, lasciviousness, idolatry, witchcraft, hatred, variance, emulations, wrath, strife, seditions, heresies, Envyings, murders, drunkenness, revellings, and such like: of the which I tell you before, as I have also told you in time past, that they which do such things shall not inherit the kingdom of God. Gal. 5:19-21

But fornication, and all uncleanness, or covetousness, let it not be once named among you, as becometh saints; neither filthiness, nor foolish talking, nor jesting, which are not convenient: but rather giving of thanks. For this ye know, that no whoremonger, nor unclean person, nor covetous man, who is an idolater, hath any inheritance in the kingdom of Christ and of God. Eph. 5:3-5

## Common Misconceptions

These verses are typically misinterpreted. Those who lean toward Arminian theology say Paul is warning believers they will lose their salvation if they persist in grievous sins, particularly sins like those listed. This view must be rejected on the preponderance of Scriptural evidence to the contrary. Believers are eternally secure.

Another common misconception is held by Calvinist-leaning theologians, who claim that those who persist in these sins demonstrate they were never saved in the first place. This view is based on the Calvinist tenet of perseverance (the "P" in the T-U-L-I-P acrostic) that insists true believers will persevere (i.e., behave) as saints throughout the Christian life, or else they are demonstrating they were never saved in the first place.

But Paul does not assume these folks are unsaved. He assumes they are saints who are continuing in sin. For example, in the Ephesians passage, he says, *Let it not be once named among you, as becometh saints*, clearly recognizing the possibility that this kind of sinful behavior can persist in the lives of genuine Christians, even if it is not appropriate. His purpose, therefore, is to issue a stiff warning: if you persist in this kind of behavior, you will not inherit the kingdom of God.

Many have taught that inheriting the kingdom of God is the equivalent to being given the gift of eternal life, but the Scriptures do not bear this out. In the context of these Pauline passages the phrase *kingdom of God* does not merely denote the eternal realm of God. It makes no sense to admonish believers to be counted worthy of the kingdom or to live in such a way so as not to forfeit the kingdom, if by *kingdom of God* he means the gift of eternal life.

No, Paul uses the phrase the *kingdom of God* in an eschatalogical sense, to refer to the millennial reign of Christ and what follows. Thus, at stake is whether believers who persist in unrighteousness will inherit the millennial reign of Christ and perhaps the eternal kingdom.

By the way, the tense of the Greek verbs in these passages is the idea of one who continues in these sins. It is not speaking of someone, who in their past, got away from God, lived for themselves and committed one or more of these sins, and then got right with God. Consider the blessed ramifications! We are not necessarily disinherited from the kingdom if we commit one of these sins. That gives great hope to us all, considering we continue with the problem of indwelling sin, even after salvation.

Thus, Paul's clear warning is that believers who persist in sin will not inherit the millennial kingdom. (Incidentally, the list of sins is not exhaustive, for Paul adds the disclaimer, *and such like*, in the Galatians passage, leaving the list open).

The key word in all these passages is *inherit*. Thayer's Greek-English Lexicon of the New Testament gives three definitions for this word that are especially helpful.

1) to receive a lot, receive by lot
2) to receive the portion assigned to one, receive an allotted portion, receive as one's own or as a possession
3) to become partaker of, to obtain

## Same Kingdom, Different Experience

For Paul to teach that persistently sinning Christians will not inherit the millennial kingdom is not the same as saying they will not be in the millennial world. All believers will be physically present in that world but apparently not all will become partakers of (or participants in) Christ's millennial kingdom. They will not inherit it. No doubt, that will result in missed opportunities, shamefulness, and much sorrow. What is clear from the Scriptures is that the millennium will not be experienced in the same way by all believers. Understandably, many Christians will be agonizing and weeping over the fact that they persisted in sins throughout their pre-millennial earthly existence. They did not appropriate the provision of Christ for living a victorious life.

Parallel to the Pauline warnings are the admonitions in the book of Hebrews. Contrary to what some may teach, the warnings are not directed toward *professing* Christians, challenging them to persevere unto salvation (in the sense of spirit-salvation, or salvation from eternal condemnation). Rather, they are warnings to actual saints to persevere unto soul-salvation, that is, perseverance unto reward. That hermeneutical key makes all the difference in interpreting the book of Hebrews. Consider the apostle's admonition:

7 Wherefore (as the Holy Ghost saith, To day if ye will hear his voice,
8 Harden not your hearts, as in the provocation, in the day of temptation in the wilderness:
9 When your fathers tempted me, proved me, and saw my works forty years.
10 Wherefore I was grieved with that generation, and said, They do alway err in their heart; and they have not known my ways.
11 So I sware in my wrath, They shall not enter into my rest).
12 Take heed, brethren, lest there be in any of you an evil heart of unbelief, in departing from the living God.
13 But exhort one another daily, while it is called To day; lest any of you be hardened through the deceitfulness of sin.
14 For we are made partakers of Christ, if we hold the beginning of our confidence stedfast unto the end; Heb. 3:7-14

The writer draws our attention to the wilderness wandering generation. They hardened their hearts, provoked Jehovah, and tested Him numerous times. So God issued a verdict (v. 11), *They shall not enter into my rest*. We know that generation did not enter into the Promised Land. They died in the wilderness. Does this imply they were unsaved and went to Hell, as some prefer to teach? No, it simply means they forfeited their conditional inheritance, which was based on obedience and faithfulness. Their unconditional inheritance, based on believing God at the Passover ensured their salvation. Jehovah was their God. They could never become disinherited from their God.

That generation of Israelites, even though they died in the wilderness and never entered the Promised Land, will be resurrected unto eternal life. They were saved people who forfeited their status as firstborn sons. They are like Christians who are *saved, yet so as by* (through) *fire*. They will be in the millennial world to come, yet they will be disinherited from ruling with Christ.

Notice how the apostle warns New Testament Christians — using the Israelites as an illustration in v. 12. He urges us to take heed, lest we develop an evil heart of unbelief. If Christians can have an evil heart of unbelief, do you suppose they can have an evil heart of covetousness or adultery or drunkenness, or any of the sins Paul lists in 1 Cor. 6, Gal. 5, or Eph. 5? Of course! That is the point.

## Beware an Evil Heart of Unbelief

Israel's evil heart of unbelief disqualified them from entering the promised rest, resulting in wandering and death in the wilderness. So you, dear Christian, if you persist in an evil heart of unbelief or other sins (as opposed to depending on God for victory) will forfeit your status as a firstborn son. In other words, you will not qualify to hear "well done," and you will not inherit the millennium. You will be disinherited at the Judgment Seat if you have not lived in obedience and faithfulness to the Word. What a tragedy to be avoided!

So what should we do? According to v. 13, we should exhort one another daily so that we do not become hardened through the deceitfulness of sin. The next verse (v. 14) gives the blessed reward for those who persevere in faithfulness. They will be made partakers of (i.e., co-participants with) Christ, both presently and in the world to come. This is a promise of rulership in Christ's kingdom. Unfortunately, some have relegated v. 14 to be a soteriological verse (that is, referring to spirit-salvation), suggesting it must be held on to or consistently demonstrated by one's life. But in context it is clearly a soul-salvation text. In other words, for those saints whose soul is presently being saved (sanctified), they are partakers (participants) with Jesus *now* and, if they continue faithful, will be deemed partakers with Him *then*.

In conclusion, the apostle issues a strong warning:

> So we see that they could not enter in because of unbelief. Let us therefore fear, lest, a promise being left us of entering into his rest, any of you should seem to come short of it. Heb. 3:19-4:1

Child of God, don't fall short of the rest God has planned for you in the age to come! Don't lose your status as firstborn son! Don't squander your millennial inheritance! If Moses could lose his inheritance in the Promised Land temporally, how much more should we take heed?

# Chapter 5

# Having a Part with Jesus

Oftentimes, God allows events and circumstances in our lives for the purpose of instructing us, impacting us, and changing our perspective. I look back on my own life at certain times when something significant occurred, and God used it to change my thinking about life and eternity. I had a paradigm shift, if you will.

In John 13 I believe Peter has a paradigm shift. His way of thinking about discipleship is radically changed, thanks to an illustration used by Jesus. Peter begins to understand a spiritual truth he had not previously grasped. His new understanding matures over the course of his life and more than thirty years later resonates from the epistles he writes as an older, wiser man. Let's first examine Peter's encounter with Jesus and then fast forward to his inspired writings.

> 1 Now before the feast of the passover, when Jesus knew that his hour was come that he should depart out of this world unto the Father, having loved his own which were in the world, he loved them unto the end.
> 4 He riseth from supper, and laid aside his garments; and took a towel, and girded himself.
> 5 After that he poureth water into a bason, and began to wash the disciples 'feet, and to wipe them with the towel wherewith he was girded.

6 Then cometh he to Simon Peter: and Peter saith unto him, Lord, dost thou wash my feet?
7 Jesus answered and said unto him, What I do thou knowest not now; but thou shalt know hereafter. John 13:1, 4-7

The context, of course, is the last supper in the upper room. Later that evening Judas would betray Jesus, resulting in His trial and crucifixion the next day. But presently Jesus is with His disciples, and because of His great love for these men, He spends several of His final hours teaching them about discipleship, preparing them for life and ministry. I marvel to think that Jesus is able to stay focused on discipling others, knowing His hour has come.

Notice the statement at the end of v. 7, *Thou shalt know hereafter.* Certainly Peter will learn more as Christ's foot-washing illustration unfolds, but it seems Jesus is pointing to the more distant future. As if to say, "Peter, you don't understand this fully right now, but one day you will understand completely."

Some commentators point out what Peter would come to understand is the importance of humility and service. Undoubtedly, that is part of the lesson. According to the parallel passage in Luke 22, the disciples had been arguing at the dinner table about who would be greatest in the kingdom. Not to mention that none of the disciples had volunteered to wash feet when they had first arrived in the upper room, though it would have been customary to wash at that time. Simply put, the disciples are too self-focused. Thus, Jesus teaches and demonstrates the importance of humility and service. And certainly Peter does come to understand that in a greater way as time passes and he matures in the Lord.

However, there is a greater truth here, I believe, that Peter needs to embrace, and it indubitably results in a paradigm shift for Peter.

Peter saith unto him, Thou shalt never wash my feet. Jesus answered him, If I wash thee not, thou hast no part with me. John 13:8

Peter protests, "You will *never* wash *my* feet!" He cannot fathom having the Messiah serve in such a lowly way. But Jesus cautions, "If you do not allow me to wash your feet, you will have no part with me." Ah! Herein lies the truth Peter must learn. To have part with Christ, a believer — for Peter is already a believer — must have clean feet, so to speak.

Peter's response is impetuous, as usual.

Simon Peter saith unto him, Lord, not my feet only, but also my hands and my head. John 13:9

Peter seems to get the point partly, but not entirely, for he blurts out, "Lord, if having a part with you requires me to be clean, then wash my entire body! I want to be in complete connection with you, Lord, so make me squeaky clean, from head to toe!" Jesus graciously and patiently continues to instruct His disciples in this truth.

Jesus saith to him, He that is washed needeth not save to wash his feet, but is clean every whit: and ye are clean, but not all. For he knew who should betray him; therefore said he, Ye are not all clean. John 13:10-11

## Two Types of Washing

From this text it becomes obvious there are two types of washing, representing two spiritual truths. The first is complete, thorough washing — head to toe — represented by the phrase, *clean every whit*. In fact, the Greek word for *washed* means completely bathed, and the tense of the verb suggests the phrase should be read, "He who has been bathed." The spiritual truth conveyed by this image is initial salvation, or justification, which transforms the spirit of man. To be *clean every whit* is to be eternally forgiven, possessing the gift of eternal life, having the spirit cleansed and regenerated. Titus 3:5 sums it up well.

Not by works of righteousness which we have done, but according to his mercy he saved us, by the washing of regeneration, and renewing of the Holy Ghost;

Eleven of the disciples in the room are clean every whit, for they have been saved. But Judas is unsaved, and that is why Jesus makes the claim, *Ye are not all clean*. So the first spiritual image is being completely washed, representing initial salva-tion or justification.

The second type of washing is simply cleansing of the feet. The word is used more than half a dozen times in John 13 and is a different Greek word than used at the beginning of v. 10 and described above. This word involves cleansing only a part, not the whole. The eleven saved men, who are already completely washed, need only to have their feet washed. In their culture, due to dusty roads and sandal-type shoes, feet would become quite dirty. Jesus is using this cultural reality to picture the temporal dirtiness we experience in our soul when we sin after we become saved. The defilement must not be allowed to remain. Sin must be confessed. In a manner of speaking, our feet must be washed regularly to cleanse away the temporal corruption of sin in our lives.

King David, after sinning with Bathsheba, cried out in confession to God, *Create in me a clean heart, O God!* In other words, "Lord, wash my dirty soul that has been tainted by sin." Of course, such sin does not affect one's eternal standing as a child of God, but it does affect one's temporal fellowship with God. Our fellowship with Him can only be restored through confession, and it can only be maintained by walking in the light as He is in the light.

> 7 But if we walk in the light, as he is in the light, we have fellow-ship one with another, and the blood of Jesus Christ his Son cleanseth us from all sin.
> 9 If we confess our sins, he is faithful and just to forgive us our sins, and to cleanse us from all unrighteousness. 1 John 1:7, 9

## A Portion With Jesus

We need to understand that Jesus was not establishing an ordinance of foot washing, nor was He merely teaching about the importance of being a servant. He was primarily giving a simple illustration that sin in the lives of saints will keep them from having a part with Christ.

It is critical that we understand this word *part* in John 13:8, for it is a key word. One of Strong's definitions of this word is an "allotment, division or share" of something. It is sometimes translated *portion* in the New Testament. In fact, when the prodigal son decided to leave home, he went to his father, and asked for his *portion of goods that falleth to me*, Luke 15:12. What was the prodigal requesting? He wanted his inheritance, his portion of the father's wealth.

Having a part with Christ is the idea of close communion and fellowship with Jesus. It is co-participation with Christ. It is becoming a joint-heir with Him and sharing His authority. Per Rom. 8:17, we know to be Christ's joint-heir requires that we suffer with Him. That is what Peter would have to learn and understand later. In fact, most Christians don't grasp that concept up front. It takes time and maturity to have part with Christ. It is the heart-cry of a mature saint, for example, the apostle Paul in Phil. 3:10-14.

## Two Spiritual Truths

In summary, Jesus illustrates two spiritual truths in John 13, using the picture of two types of washing:

**1. Washing of the whole person** — representing the regeneration of your spirit, which occurred instantaneously at the point of initial salvation, when you believed on Christ and passed from death unto life. It is eternal and, therefore, cannot be repeated.

**2. Washing of the feet only** — representing cleansing from sin after salvation, in your soul, when you confess sin, so that your fellowship with God is restored. When your feet are clean, you are walking in the light and the blood of Jesus continues to keep you cleansed in a sanctification sense. But if you, dear Christian, do not continue to have your feet washed — if you continue to live in sin — then your fellowship with God is marred and your soul is not being saved. You will lose your soul, that is, your reward, at the Judgment Seat. You do not now, and will not then, have part with Christ. You will not co-participate with Him in his kingdom. The bottom line: you will not inherit the kingdom. What a lesson for Peter and the other disciples!

Did Peter catch the truth as illustrated by Jesus in footwashing? To answer that question, we must explore Peter's epistles, starting with 1 Peter.

3 Blessed be the God and Father of our Lord Jesus Christ, which according to his abundant mercy hath begotten us again unto a lively hope by the resurrection of Jesus Christ from the dead,
4 To an inheritance incorruptible, and undefiled, and that fadeth not away, reserved in heaven for you,
5 Who are kept by the power of God through faith unto salvation ready to be revealed in the last time.
6 Wherein ye greatly rejoice, though now for a season, if need be, ye are in heaviness through manifold temptations:
7 That the trial of your faith, being much more precious than of gold that perisheth, though it be tried with fire, might be found unto praise and honour and glory at the appearing of Jesus Christ:
8 Whom having not seen, ye love; in whom, though now ye see him not, yet believing, ye rejoice with joy unspeakable and full of glory:
9 Receiving the end of your faith, even the salvation of your souls.
1 Pet. 1:3-9

## Inheritance Incorruptible — Conditional or Unconditional?

We know from the previous chapter, there are two inheritances in the Scriptures. One is unconditional and refers to our eternal standing — we are children of God and, since children, then heirs. But the other is conditional, based on our spiritual works for Christ. If we are faithful, then we are considered inheritors of the kingdom, firstborn sons, co-heirs with Christ, in the sense that we will rule with Him in His coming kingdom. Thus, in every scripture passage where inheritance is mentioned, we must look contextually and see how it is being used — whether in the unconditional sense or in a conditional sense.

Upon first glance, the *inheritance incorruptible* in v. 4 appears to be unconditional, for all saints. But I do not believe that is the case, as I hope to demonstrate. What often confuses people is the phrase at the end of v. 4, *reserved in heaven for you*. The tendency is to assume that phrase is referring to eternal life. However, the reward is not Heaven, per se; the reward is *reserved* (i.e., held) in Heaven for the faithful. It is something other than Heaven itself. Jesus made this clear in the Gospels:

Lay not up for yourselves treasures upon earth, where moth and rust doth corrupt, and where thieves break through and steal: But lay up for yourselves treasures in heaven. Matt. 6:19-20

Treasures on Earth do not refer to Earth itself, but rather to things that people value and store up on Earth. Obviously, these treasures are not available to everyone. For instance, your bank account cannot be accessed by me or anyone else. So treasures in Heaven do not refer to Heaven itself, but rather to rewards that Christians value and store up in the eternal realm that will not be available to all. They are reserved for the one who stores them up. Incidentally, laying up treasures in Heaven has nothing to do with initial salvation of one's spirit. If it did, then salvation would be by works. Storing up treasures in Heaven is a sanctification concept, a matter of salvation of the soul. In the text in 1 Peter, we find at least five evidences that inheritance in this particular passage is conditional.

### Evidences of Conditional Inheritance

**1. According to v. 9, soul-salvation is in view** — *receiving the ... salvation of your souls.* The salvation focus in this passage is not the eternal salvation of the spirit that occurred in the past; it is the progressive salvation/sanctification of the soul that culminates in the future, resulting in reward. It is what one receives. The word *receives* carries the idea of obtaining that which one rightly deserves, as demonstrated in the following verses where the same word is also used:

> For we must all appear before the judgment seat of Christ; that every one may **receive** the things done in his body, according to that he hath done, whether it be good or bad. 2 Cor. 5:10

> But he that doeth wrong shall **receive** for the wrong which he hath done: and there is no respect of persons. Col. 3:25

> For ye have need of patience, that, after ye have done the will of God, ye might **receive** the promise. Heb. 10:36

> And when the chief Shepherd shall appear, ye shall **receive** a crown of glory that fadeth not away. 1 Pet. 5:4

**2. The reward is conditioned upon your faith** — *receiving the end of your faith.* The reward is the climax of a life of dependence on God. The word *end* means goal or consummation. It is the same basic word used by Jesus on the cross, when He cried out, "It is finished!" The end had come; the goal had been reached. The end of salvation for Christians is the Judgment Seat. At that time, our works will be judged and rewards will be given. The end of a faith-filled life will be positive reward, whereas the end of an unfaithful life will be negative reward, as we shall see in the next chapter.

3. **The reward is contingent on enduring through sufferings** — *That the trial of your faith ... might be found unto praise and honour and glory at the appearing of Jesus Christ.* This clearly demonstrates that the Judgment Seat and rewards, not a so-called ticket to Heaven, are Peter's focal point. Notice that rewards are based on enduring in suffering. Other Scripture passages corroborate this point also.

> And if children, then heirs; heirs of God, and joint- heirs with Christ; if so be that we suffer with him, that we may be also glorified together. Rom. 8:17

> If we suffer, we shall also reign with him: if we deny him, he also will deny us: 2 Tim. 2:12

It is the trying of our faith that produces patience (endurance), according to James 1:2-4. If we cooperate with God in our suffering, having a sweet, enduring spirit, He will make us complete and mature, ready to meet Him at the Judgment Seat. Those saints who have endured their fiery trials on Earth will be equipped to endure the Judgment Seat fires (1 Cor. 3:13-15). To endure does not mean simply to make it through. To endure is to bear up under the pressure with joyfulness. *Count it all joy when ye fall into divers temptations,* James 1:2. Those who do will *be found unto praise and honor and glory,* 1 Pet. 1:7, when Christ appears. Those who do not endure their sufferings will be ashamed, the very thing John warns about in 1 John 2:28.

4. **The reward is conditional in v. 5.** Our tendency is to put a period at the end of v. 4, but that is incorrect. *To an inheritance incorruptible ... reserved in heaven for you.* But the sentence does not end there. It continues on into v. 5. The inheritance is *reserved in heaven for you who are kept by the power of God through faith unto salvation.* It is only for those who live by faith and are, therefore, kept or preserved by God's power

unto soul-salvation at the Bema. Those who are not preserved by God's power, through faith, will be ashamed; they will receive a negative reward.

**5. Peter admonishes, not merely to look forward to Heaven, but to prepare for the Judgment Seat.**

> Wherefore gird up the loins of your mind, be sober, and hope to the end for the grace that is to be brought unto you at the revelation of Jesus Christ; As obedient children, not fashioning yourselves according to the former lusts in your ignorance: But as he which hath called you is holy, so be ye holy in all manner of conversation; Because it is written, Be ye holy; for I am holy. 1 Pet. 1:13-16

How are we to prepare? First, by getting sober about life and the prospect of meeting Jesus at the Judgment Seat. Second, by hoping — confidently anticipating — the grace Christ will bestow at His judgment bar. Incidentally, this is not looking backward to the grace by which you were saved. It is looking forward to the grace by which you will be rewarded. God is loving and gracious to shower His grace upon those who are faithful, though we do not deserve it. Third, we prepare by leaving off the old life of lust and living holy unto the Lord. Interestingly, the word *holy* in the Greek is the same basic word as *sanctification*.

Much more could be said about this passage, but the main point is that it is a sanctification text, resulting in reward for the faithful, a salvation-of-the-soul text (1 Pet. 1:9), not a salvation-from-eternal-damnation text. Here we have Peter, thirty-plus years after having his feet washed by Jesus, now understanding the concept of having a part with Christ and receiving an inheritance incorruptible. This inheritance is not the portion that will be received by all Christians, for all Christians have not chosen to participate with Christ. Many have no part with Christ in the sense of fellowship and so at the Judgment Seat will be ashamed.

The concept of a conditional inheritance so resonated with Peter that he thought it important to bring up again in his second epistle. The passage (2 Pet. 1) starts with positional sanctification, which gives our provision in Christ (v. 3), then it moves to practical or progressive sanctification (v. 4-9). Finally, it culminates in the Judgment Seat (v. 10-11).

According as his divine power hath given unto us all things that pertain unto life and godliness, through the knowledge of him that hath called us to glory and virtue: 2 Pet. 1:3

## Positional Sanctification — the Provision

*His divine power* is the Holy Spirit of God who lives within our spirit. He has given to us everything we need for spiritual liveliness and godliness through our relationship-knowledge of Christ. The Greek implies it is mature, intimate, personal, experiential knowledge. Christ lives in us (Gal. 2:20) through His blessed Holy Spirit, and thus we have the complete provision for a life of victory. What a marvelous thought! The apostle John said it even more emphatically:

Whosoever is born of God doth not commit sin; for his seed remaineth in him: and he cannot sin, because he is born of God. 1 John 3:9

Of course, John is speaking of the spirit-realm of man's being, not the soul-realm. The word *seed* in the Greek is *sperma* and conveys the idea that God's own divine seed is implanted in our spirit when we are saved. Because of that, we cannot sin in our spirit-realm, because we are born of God. Glory! Hallelujah! The problem is not that we have inadequate provision. The problem is that we do not appropriate in our soul what we have in Christ in our spirit.

Peter continues on in v. 4 to speak of progressive sanctification and the means of becoming holy.

Whereby are given unto us exceeding great and precious promises: that by these ye might be partakers of the divine nature, having escaped the corruption that is in the world through lust. 2 Pet. 1:4

## Progressive Sanctification — the Outworking

Peter changes his focus from the provision in our spirit — positional sanctification (v. 3) — to the practical outworking in our lives — ongoing sanctification, the salvation of the soul. Made obvious in this text is the fact that progressing in holiness is by no means guaranteed. It is a cooperative program of working out your own salvation (Phil. 2:12), while depending on God who is working in your life to sanctify you (Phil. 2:13). Every believer must choose to cooperate with God on a continual basis.

Peter tells us that happens when we claim the exceeding great and precious promises, which are at our disposal in the Word of God. Faith claims those promises and depends on the Lord for victory. Literally, by claiming the promises we become participants in Christ's nature and escape the corruptions of the world and its lusts. This is the formula for victory. It is the only way the soul can be saved — or, we could say, progressively sanctified — and it is the only thing that will survive at the Judgment Seat.

> And beside this, giving all diligence, add to your faith virtue; and to virtue knowledge; And to knowledge temperance; and to temperance patience; and to patience godliness; And to godliness brotherly kindness; and to brotherly kindness charity. 2 Pet. 1:5-7

Peter goes on in v. 5 to say, *and beside all this,* — or "for this very reason" — *add to your faith.* In the context, the faith here is not saving faith; it is sanctifying faith. It is the same kind of faith that claims the promises mentioned in v. 4. But the Christian life is not only about faith; it's also about hope and love (1 Cor. 13:13). So to progress onward in the Christian life we must choose to cooperate diligently with God's sanctification program in our lives, letting Him develop the graces of a Spirit-filled life. They include:

- Virtue — moral excellence
- Knowledge — a growing understanding of God through His Word
- Temperance — control of self (body, thoughts, emotions, passions, etc.)
- Patience — perseverance amidst trials
- Godliness — a God-like soul
- Brotherly kindness — treating others as you treat yourself
- Love — treating others as God treats you

This is the result of progressive sanctification, in a nutshell. Rom. 5:1-5 is a parallel text that we will explore in Chapter 12. We come at last to the climax, and it is truly glorious.

> For if these things be in you, and abound, they make you that ye shall neither be barren nor unfruitful in the knowledge of our Lord Jesus Christ. 2 Pet. 1:8

What a promise! Incidentally, this is what survives the testing furnace at the Judgment Seat. In contradistinction, look at the contrast in the following verse:

> But he that lacketh these things is blind, and cannot see afar off, and hath forgotten that he was purged from his old sins. 2 Pet. 1:9

The result of a flesh-dependent life, that does not claim the promises and thereby appropriate the provision of Christ within, is defeat now and shame at the Judgment Seat. The soul will be forfeited, the works consumed, the reward lost. For those who depend on the Spirit of God, however, they will share in Christ's divine nature and escape the world's corruption. Their inheritance reward will be great.

> Wherefore the rather, brethren, give diligence to make your calling and election sure: for if ye do these things, ye shall never fall: 2 Pet. 1:10

## Called and Elected Unto Sanctification

Some like to make this a salvation-from-Hell verse, insisting, based on the phrase, *Make your calling and election sure*, v. 10, that a person is not actually saved unless they demonstrate these things in some degree in their lives. That is not what the passage is teaching, as we have demonstrated. The calling and election referred to in this verse are not unto salvation of our spirit but unto sanctification of our soul. Two verses from the Pauline epistles bear this out:

> For whom he did foreknow, he also did predestinate to be conformed to the image of his Son, that he might be the firstborn among many brethren. Rom. 8:29

> According as he hath chosen us in him before the foundation of the world, that we should be holy and without blame before him in love: Eph. 1:4

Our calling and election are not unto salvation but unto holiness. That was Peter's point also in 1 Pet. 1:15-16, which we noted earlier.

So here's the point of 2 Pet. 1:10: *Make your calling and election sure.* Putting it another way, keep your feet clean. When you do, by cooperating with God and letting Him do His full sanctifying work in your life, your reward will be sure and stable. You will pass through the fires of the Judgment Seat safely, not losing your soul. The glorious conclusion is given in v. 11.

> For so an entrance shall be ministered unto you abundantly into the everlasting kingdom of our Lord and Saviour Jesus Christ. 2 Pet. 1:11

This is the reward for overcomers — abundant entrance into the kingdom of Christ, the nature of which will be discussed in a later chapter.

Peter was so impacted by the foot-washing illustration of Jesus that he never forgot the critical importance of having a part with Jesus, conditional inheritance with Him. Peter wrote about it in both of his epistles, and he apparently reminded people of these truths repeatedly, for much is at stake.

> Wherefore I will not be negligent to put you always in remembrance of these things, though ye know them, and be established in the present truth. Yea, I think it meet, as long as I am in this tabernacle, to stir you up by putting you in remembrance ... Moreover I will endeavour that ye may be able after my decease to have these things always in remembrance. 2 Pet. 1:12-13,15

Peter admonishes his readers to continue teaching this truth even after his death. Yet, ironically, this is one of the most neglected doctrines in the church of Jesus Christ. One of the major purposes of this book is to call the attention of saints to this important Bible doctrine.

# Chapter 6

# Possible Verdicts at the Bema

What do most Christians think about future judgment? I read a statement recently on a Bible question-and-answer website that represents the naive understanding of orthodox Christianity. *(Note: I have chosen not to reveal the sources for the quotes below, so as not to hurt the parties involved, although they are actual quotes).*

> God will judge everyone, both believers and non-believers. The non-believers will be cast into the lake of fire, but the believers are saved and will go to heaven. Although we are saved, we will be judged, not to determine if we'll go to heaven, but to determine how many rewards we'll get. God will determine how many rewards to give us in heaven, and what position we'll have in heaven. But we will all be in the presence of God, and we'll all be happy.

Here's another similar statement taken from a dispensationalist newsletter:

> In heaven, the redeemed will be equal in Christ. All our tears and infirmities will be gone. All of us will have a heavenly mansion. We will all possess a body like Christ's body. We will all finally be able to gaze upon the face of God in all His fullness. Each one of us will possess these gifts and so much more.

In essence, these statements are saying we'll all live happily-ever-after in Heaven with Jesus. Everything will be hunky-dory. No mention is made of the possibility of a negative verdict at the Judgment Seat and no mention is made of how our lifestyle in the coming kingdom of Christ will be contingent on how we live our lives in this present world.

With theology like this, where's the motivation to deny self, take up your cross, and follow Him? Discipleship is painful. Why bother to pay the price of discipleship if everyone is going to receive the same and be treated the same in the age to come? Does not this kind of theology subtly condone licentious living? Is it any wonder, then, that twenty-first century Christians don't have a fear of God? Is it any wonder that Christians live for self and that they are full of the world? After all, if there are no serious consequences, why emphasize discipleship? If we're all going to enjoy the blessings of Heaven rather equally, why bother? No one would articulate it that way, of course, but that's the bottom line. When the seriousness of the Judgment Seat is downplayed, everyone expects to be rewarded. Everyone thinks they will have a mansion. Nothing could be further from the truth.

## Positive and Negative Reward

Unfortunately, many Christians assume that all born-again believers will be rewarded at the Judgment Seat of Christ — some more, some less. Oh, there may be a moment of regret or agony, but it will not be ongoing and will be quickly forgotten. They arrive at this conclusion in spite of the clear language of Scripture.

> Every man's work shall be made manifest: for the day shall declare it, because it shall be revealed by fire; and the fire shall try every man's work of what sort it is. If any man's work abide which he hath built thereupon, he shall receive a reward. If any man's work shall be burned, he shall suffer loss: but he himself shall be saved; yet so as by fire. 1 Cor. 3:13-15

The mistake often made is interpreting the phrase *suffer loss* as not receiving as many positive rewards as someone else. The interpretation is based on an assumption that since believers are positionally righteous, our sins can never be judged and, therefore, nothing of a serious negative nature will be dealt with at the Judgment Seat. According to this popular view, the Bema will essentially be an awards ceremony for dispensing trophies. Is that accurate?

"Suffering loss" at the Judgment Seat is not merely receiving fewer positive rewards; it is the idea of being recompensed for the wrong one has done. It is a setback, a payback of negative reward. In fact, the two words in English, *suffer loss*, are actually one word in Greek, and the word means "to injure, to experience detriment; to be cast away, to receive damage" (Strong). Heb. 10:29 uses the word *punishment* to describe the negative reward, and Strong says *punishment* is penalty. That's a radically different understanding than what many Christians have about the Judgment Seat. Perhaps there will be shock and surprise for many at the rapture.

The Scriptures very clearly confirm the prospect of negative reward at the Judgment Seat.

> And whatsoever ye do, do it heartily, as to the Lord, and not unto men; Knowing that of the Lord ye shall receive the reward of the inheritance: for ye serve the Lord Christ. But he that doeth wrong shall receive for the wrong which he hath done: and there is no respect of persons. Col. 3:23-25

In addition to the prospect of a negative reward, the passage above indicates another possibility at the Judgment Seat will be receiving *the reward of the inheritance*, which is positive. The point, as we learned in the previous chapters, is that inheriting millennial blessings is not automatic. Incidentally, the fact that God shows *no respect of persons* does not mean all will receive the same recompense. Rather, it means *all* will be recompensed accordingly. God does not play politics.

## Servants Awaiting Their Lord's Return

Jesus shared a parable with His disciples, illustrating the truth of positive or negative reward for believers. We will first examine the parable, then the application.

35 Let your loins be girded about, and your lights burning;
36 And ye yourselves like unto men that wait for their lord, when he will return from the wedding; that when he cometh and knocketh, they may open unto him immediately.
41 Then Peter said unto him, Lord, speakest thou this parable unto us, or even to all? Luke 12:35-36, 41

Jesus often spoke in parables to reveal truth about the kingdom to those who were ready and eager to receive it, and to conceal truth about the kingdom from those who were blind and hard-hearted. The disciples were in the former group, and the Pharisees and chief priests in the latter. Thus, we have part of the answer to Peter's question *in* his question. From Christ's answer, it becomes obvious that He was speaking primarily to His disciples. In fact, the reader is explicitly told this in Luke 12:1, 22. By extension, Jesus is speaking to all saved people, and that includes us. His will is that all saved people go all the way through in discipleship and be rewarded in the judgment. Keep in mind that disciples are not merely saved people. Disciples are saved people who have chosen to follow Jesus, no matter what the cost. To that end, Jesus shares this parable to motivate us to live in such a manner that we will be able to give a good account to Him one day in the future.

In order to understand the parable in the verses above, it is important to first grasp the main point of Christ's teaching, which He gives in v. 36. He wants us to be like servants who are awaiting their Lord's return, ready to open the door immediately when He knocks. In the next verse, He calls those servants *blessed*. This parable cannot be referring to lost people, because lost people would not be pictured as awaiting their Lord's return; that is only true of saved people.

In what respect are servants of Christ to be awaiting His return? Jesus does not leave us wondering. We must consider the context:

> But rather seek ye the kingdom of God; and all these things shall be added unto you. Fear not, little flock; for it is your Father's good pleasure to give you the kingdom. Sell that ye have, and give alms; provide yourselves bags which wax not old, a treasure in the heavens that faileth not, where no thief approacheth, neither moth corrupteth. For where your treasure is, there will your heart be

also. Let your loins be girded about, and your lights burning. Luke 12:31-35

Jesus wants His servants to be seeking His coming kingdom diligently, knowing that His desire is to give it to us. Giving us the kingdom is a concept that will be explained in a later chapter in this book. Furthermore, Christ wants us not to have the focus that this world is our home, but rather that we are mere pilgrims on Earth, awaiting our heavenly home. The way multitudes of Christians live, it is obvious they do not have this focus. They are attached to the here and now and spend their money on material things rather than eternal causes. Finally, Jesus wants our loins to be girded about and our lights burning (undoubtedly a reference to the parable of the ten virgins in Matt. 25). In a spiritual sense, Jesus wants His disciples to be detached from the world, not ashamed at the rapture, ready to meet Him at the Judgment Seat. Are you truly ready to give a good account?

It is obvious throughout the parable that Jesus is speaking to saved people because He repeatedly refers to servants and their lord (master). Christ is not the Lord of unsaved people. Rather, Satan, the god of this world, is their master. Indeed, an unsaved person can never make Christ the Lord of his life. Saved people, on the other hand, are servants of Christ by default, so this parable applies to all who are born-again children of God.

## The Faithful Servant

Jesus promises we will be blessed if we are faithfully awaiting His return. In fact, He promises to gird Himself and serve His faithful servants!

> Blessed are those servants, whom the lord when he cometh shall find watching: verily I say unto you, that he shall gird himself, and make them to sit down to meat, and will come forth and serve them. And if he shall come in the second watch, or come in the third watch, and find them so, blessed are those servants. Luke 12:37-38

How does a faithful servant act? He is prepared for the Master's return by being a wise steward and managing his

Master's affairs obediently and responsibly and by serving the Master faithfully (i.e., full of faith). He does not live like the rich fool, consumed with the here and now — see the parable in Luke 12:16-21 (incidentally, this parable refers to believers). The faithful servant looks not at things that are seen, but at things that are not seen (2 Cor. 4:18). His life is about seeking first the kingdom of God. He bears fruit. He does not live unto himself, but unto Him who died for him. This Christian is a living sacrifice, holy, acceptable unto God. He has counted the cost and paid the price of discipleship.

In contrast, the return of Christ will come as a thief in the night for those who are not ready, those who have lived for self.

> And this know, that if the goodman of the house had known what hour the thief would come, he would have watched, and not have suffered his house to be broken through. Be ye therefore ready also: for the Son of man cometh at an hour when ye think not. Luke 12:39-40

While unfaithful Christians will be shocked at Christ's return, those who are faithful servants will be expecting His "knock" at their door, so to speak. The parable is clear (in later verses) that the unfaithful will be punished while the faithful will be handsomely rewarded. The reward for faithfulness is more than we could imagine!

> And the Lord said, Who then is that faithful and wise steward, whom his lord shall make ruler over his household, to give them their portion of meat in due season? Blessed is that servant, whom his lord when he cometh shall find so doing ... he will make him ruler over all that he hath. Luke 12:42-44

The faithful steward is rewarded, for his works are deemed to be of the caliber of gold, silver, and precious stones. He will hear, *Well done, good and faithful servant*. He will rule and reign with Christ in His coming kingdom. That is not true of unfaithful servants.

Every child of God ought to take heed to the warning of Christ in v. 40, *Be ye therefore ready also: for the Son of man cometh at an hour when ye think not*. Are you doing what the Master expects of you? Are you depending on the Spirit of

God for living the Christ life of victory? One day you will give an account. While the reward for faithfulness is unfathomable (in a positive sense), the reward for unfaithfulness is overwhelming (in a negative sense).

After describing the wonderful blessings given for faithfulness, Jesus then turns our attention to the aspect of negative recompense for unfaithful servants.

> 45 But and if that servant say in his heart, My lord delayeth his coming; and shall begin to beat the menservants and maidens, and to eat and drink, and to be drunken;
> 46 The lord of that servant will come in a day when he looketh not for him, and at an hour when he is not aware, and will cut him in sunder, and will appoint him his portion with the unbelievers.
> 47 And that servant, which knew his lord's will, and prepared not himself, neither did according to his will, shall be beaten with many stripes.
> 48 But he that knew not, and did commit things worthy of stripes, shall be beaten with few stripes. For unto whomsoever much is given, of him shall be much required: and to whom men have committed much, of him they will ask the more. Luke 12:45-48

When considering the dramatic application of the parable, we need to be aware of three important facts. First, parables are intended to be metaphorical in nature. Some Christians react rather violently to the prospect of a child of God being *cut asunder* or *beaten with many stripes*, concluding that such harsh treatment could never be the lot of a saved person. Thus, they instantly assume the unfaithful servants in the parable must be referring to those who are unsaved. As we shall see, the entire parable applies to the saved, and one of the keys to interpretation is understanding that parabolic language is figurative.

Second, throughout the parable Jesus repeatedly refers to *that servant* and *his lord* (master) — see v. 42-43, 45-47. The *Lord* is obviously Christ and the *servant* is a saved person. Unsaved people are never referred to as servants of Christ.

Third, the repeated use of the phrase *that servant* clearly indicates that Jesus is not referring to four different people (one saved, three unsaved, or some other combination). Instead, this is one — and only one — servant, who has four possible lifestyle choices and, consequently, four possible rewards at the Judgment Seat.

## The Rebellious Servant

The second possible lifestyle a Christian can choose is rebellion to the Lord in some degree. In this particular parable Jesus describes an extreme servant who mistreats those under his care (beats them) and indulges himself (becomes drunken). The parable is clear that this servant behaves thusly because he rationalizes, *My lord delayeth his coming.* In other words, he is not convinced that Jesus is coming any time soon. He doesn't take seriously the eternal realm. He is more focused on the here and now.

Some may wonder, "How could this be a Christian? No Christian would do this kind of thing!" Oh really? Do you know any Christians that get drunk or abuse drugs? Do you know any Christians who are abusive? Do you know any Christians who live in adultery? Do you know any Christians who have major outbursts of anger? Do you know any Christians who, because of continued selfishness, have destroyed their marriage and family? Do you know any Christians who live like the devil? Do you know any Christians that deny their Lord? In a Bible sense, think Lot, think Peter, think Ananias and Sapphira, to name a few.

Yes, even Christians can live carnally for a period of time or even a lifetime. Passages like Rom. 7 and the books of 1 Cor. and Heb. demonstrate the possibility. That is why God disciplines His children who are living rebelliously. *Whom the Lord loves He chastens,* Heb. 12:6. Incidentally, those being disciplined do not always respond favorably – and so we are given strong warnings in Heb. 12:25, *See that ye refuse not Him that speaketh,* and Heb. 12:29, *Our God is a consuming fire.*

If God disciplines and judges now, why wouldn't He do so at the Judgment Seat, of all places? *Judgment must begin at the house of God,* 1 Pet. 4:17. Indeed, the very idea of a Judgment Seat suggests that some do not live as they should on Earth and so will give an account to Jesus.

How do we explain the awful punishment of the rebellious servant, who is *cut asunder?* Remember, this is a parable. God doesn't literally hack him in pieces. Even if this punishment were literal, it would be inconsistent with the crime of abusiveness and drunkenness. It would not be an eye-for-an-eye type punishment.

*Cut asunder* comes from the Greek word *dichotomeo*, from which we get our English word *dichotomy*. It is the idea of dividing something into two equal parts. This appears to be a metaphor for the sword of the Spirit, which is the word of God, severely rebuking the rebellious servant. In Rev. 19:15 we are told that from the mouth of the Lord Jesus comes a sharp sword. In other words, His words cut and divide and separate. In Heb. 4:12 we learn:

> For the word of God is quick, and powerful, and sharper than any two-edged sword, piercing even to the dividing asunder of soul and spirit, and of the joints and marrow, and is a discerner of the thoughts and intents of the heart.

Why would God want to divide asunder one of His rebellious children in this manner? Think of it. The spirit of even a rebellious child of God is righteous. But the soul (mind, will, emotions) of a saint who is not submitting to ongoing sanctification is far from righteous. Perhaps Jesus — through strong rebuke — divides apart the righteous spirit from the corrupt soul in order to fully make manifest to His rebellious child the awfulness of his heart.

> Every man's work shall be made manifest. 1 Cor. 3:13

> The Lord ... will bring to light the hidden things of darkness, and will make manifest the counsels of the hearts. 1 Cor. 4:5

Imagine the horror of standing at the Judgment Seat and hearing Jesus, the living Word of God, divide between your soul and spirit so you can see your innermost being. You will no longer cling to the argument that since you are saved, born-again, justified, and positionally righteous you should not, therefore, be judged. For your soul will be exposed independently of the spirit, and all of your behavioral corruption will be made manifest. Then imagine the awfulness of the verdict as the fire of God's judgment burns away all that is corrupt, leaving nothing. If that were all of the punishment, it would be horrid enough, but that is not all.

The rebellious servant is also appointed *his portion with the unbelievers,* Luke 12:46. This punishment, at face value, has prompted many an unwitting interpreter — despite the many textual evidences to the contrary — to conclude that the rebellious servant is consigned to an eternity in Hell. But the passage does not say that. In fact, the word translated *unbelievers* here is often translated *faithless* elsewhere in the New Testament. So it doesn't have to mean an unsaved person. It can legitimately refer to an unbelieving Christian, and context determines the usage. When Jesus met Thomas on the day of his resurrection, and Thomas doubted, Jesus used this very Greek word to describe Thomas, calling him *faithless,* John 20:27, in the sense of lacking faith.

In the context of Luke 12, we must interpret this usage as an unbelieving *Christian;* in other words, a Christian who is not depending on God for victory. He is faithless, like Thomas, living in defeat. He is saved, but he is not trusting God to live a holy life. Thus, his life is displeasing to his Master, and he will be recompensed at the Judgment Seat. This servant is the opposite of the faithful servant in v. 42.

Incidentally, the faithless servant is appointed a *portion.* A *portion* is an allotment or share. Unlike the faithful servant, who receives blessing and ruling and reigning with Christ, the portion of the faithless servant is no opportunity to rule or reign, a very mundane form of existence in the kingdom, and no blessing.

In addition, according to the parallel passage, the rebellious servant's punishment results in *weeping and gnashing of teeth,* Matt. 24:51. Unfortunately, many Bible teachers have relegated that phrase to suffering in Hell. However, in oriental thinking, gnashing of teeth is simply conscious regret. That's all it means! A person could gnash his teeth because he is in Hell, and consciously regretting it, or a person could gnash his teeth because he receives punishment at the Judgment Seat, and it affects his existence in the coming kingdom, and he consciously regrets it! It is unwise to let a phrase determine the interpretation of an entire passage. Rather, one should let the passage dictate the way the phrase is being used.

Imagine being harshly rebuked by Jesus at the Judgment Seat, seeing your soul for what it really is, not receiving any rewards, and having to live in a realm of the kingdom without an inheritance, frequently weeping and regretting the fact that you did not live for God in this life. This is serious! It would be worse than Isaiah crying, *Woe is me! For I am undone; for I am a man of unclean lips,* Isa. 6:5. It would be worse than Peter crying, *Depart from me; for I am a sinful man, O Lord,* Luke 5:8. It would be worse than Job crying, *I abhor myself,* Job 42:6.

## The Indifferent Servant

Perhaps you are relieved that your lifestyle is not represented by the rebellious servant, but are you acting as an indifferent servant, focusing on self and forgetting about the return of Christ and the world to come?

According to v. 47, this servant knows His Lord's will but does not live accordingly. I personally think this servant describes the vast majority of western Christianity. We know what God expects of us. We are well-taught people. But many dispensational Christians have been taught that the Judgment Seat will involve a few moments of pain, then it will be over and all will be joyful in the kingdom to come. *Not so!*

Those who do not have an eternal focus will be beaten with many stripes. Again, this is a parable; the stripes are figurative. In Heb. 12 we are told whom the Lord loves He scourges. Have you ever been literally flogged by God? No, scourging is a metaphor for God's divine discipline in your life. He sends appropriate punishments when you are living unto yourself, in order that He might get your attention and turn your heart completely to Him. Sometimes those punishments continue on for a lengthy period of time, perhaps even years. The punishments dispensed at the Judgment Seat are even more consequential, the results lasting at least throughout the millennial kingdom age, and more likely, eternally. *(Note: I lean to the position that rewards are eternal, both positive and negative, e.g., see Ps. 103:17; Dan. 12:2-3; Heb. 5:9; Rev. 22:5. However, a discussion of this subject is beyond the scope of this present book.)*

Are you indifferent to your Lord's return? Are you living for yourself? Are you materialistic? Are you bearing fruit for the Master? Have you left your first love? Do you have a form of godliness but deny the power thereof? Will you be punished at His Judgment Seat?

## The Ignorant Servant

We find one final type of servant in v. 48. This servant is also beaten, but not as intensely as the indifferent servant, because this servant is ignorant. I personally do not think this last punishment will apply to anyone reading this book. Because you have been warned. Indeed, I think the church in the western world has largely been warned, even if it has unwittingly arrived at incorrect interpretations of many passages, such as this very parable. To whom much is given, much is required. If anything, I suppose this last type of servant would apply to those reared in a context where they had no access to biblical teaching. Perhaps this would apply to those overseas who get saved but have little opportunity for discipleship. Maybe they don't even have their own copy of the Bible. I cannot fathom that ignorance will be a valid excuse for western Christians at the Judgment Seat.

Will your reward at the Judgment Seat be positive or negative? If negative, do you realize what that means? It means forfeiture of kingdom inheritance. It means you will not take full possession of the glories and blessings of the kingdom as you could have. Though you will be in the kingdom as a child of God, your portion will be among the faithless. It means you will not glow with the brightness of the Savior. It's time that Christians awake to righteousness! Jesus is coming soon!

## For the Jews Only?

Some like to dismiss this passage as referring to the Jews exclusively, and claim it has no bearing on New Testament Christians. Unfortunately, they do that with many passages in the Gospels (inconsistently), insisting the pre-cross era of Christ was a different dispensation and, therefore, not applicable to the church. Does this mean the Gospels are merely history books with no practical application for New Testament believers? God forbid! Jesus said, *The law and the prophets were until John,* Luke 16:16. He did not say the era of law would end abruptly at the cross. While we recognize the importance of dispensations, it is possible to press them too hard, so that dispensationalism (as a system) may be guilty of putting the Scriptures in a box that God never intended.

In response to this Jewish-only hermeneutic (system of interpretation), we would give two key responses. First, when the Jewish leadership rejected the kingdom offer, Jesus took the kingdom from national Israel and gave it to another *nation bringing forth the fruits thereof,* Matt. 21:43. We recognize the other "nation" to be the church. Thus the qualifications for kingdom entrance given to the Jews in the Gospels are also for the saints of the church age.

Second, since the Jewish leadership apostatized, Jesus turned to His disciples — those who had chosen to follow Him no matter the cost. With them He continued teaching about the kingdom (see Acts 1:3). While those disciples were Jewish, they were also Christians. In fact, the twelve chosen by Jesus (Judas was later replaced) became the foundation of the local church, according to Eph. 2:20, and they will sit on twelve thrones in the kingdom (Matt. 19:28). As Christians — Jewish or not — it would make sense for Jesus to instruct them about the rapture, the Judgment Seat of Christ, and the coming kingdom. That being the case, I would submit that Jesus' teaching in the Gospels is for our admonition as much as it was for the first century Jewish believers.

## Conclusion

The traditional understanding of the Judgment Seat of Christ assumes only one basic verdict for all saints: positive reward (in some measure). The Bema is viewed as an awards podium. However, the Scriptures actually teach the prospect of two possible verdicts: positive reward for the faithful or negative reward for the unfaithful, depending on one's service to the Master. The Scriptures sometimes refer to negative reward as *suffer loss, recompense,* or simply *punishment.*

# Chapter 7

# Judged for Sinning?

Will the sins we commit after salvation be judged at the Judgment Seat of Christ? Some say an emphatic, "No!" because our sins are completely covered under the blood of Calvary. Some say an emphatic, "Yes!" because the nature of Christ's judgment of our sins at the Bema is not legal, as if to determine our position in Him, but rather it is disciplinary, like a father determining the necessary punishment for his child's misbehavior. Others say, "Yes and no," and some aren't sure. But what saith the Scriptures?

To those who say, "Absolutely not; our sins cannot be judged at the Judgment Seat, for they are under the blood," let me remind that God sometimes judges sin in the lives of believers in this present era. Assuming my assertion can be substantiated from the Scriptures, then what would keep Him from judging sin at the Bema? After all, we are under the blood just as much now as then. So if He judges sin now, He will surely judge it then.

My first order of business in this chapter will be to demonstrate a) that God does, indeed, judge sin in this present age and b) that it will culminate at the Judgment Seat. Second, I wish to point out there are two levels of sinning and therefore two levels of judging, not merely one. Distinguishing between the levels may help some to understand

how God can judge sin even after a person becomes a child of
God.

## Eight Ways God Judges Sin Now

### 1. God does not listen to the prayers of saints who continue in known sin.

> If I regard iniquity in my heart, the Lord will not hear me: Ps. 66:18

> Behold, the Lord's hand is not shortened, that it cannot save;
> neither his ear heavy, that it cannot hear: But your iniquities have
> separated between you and your God, and your sins have hid his
> face from you, that he will not hear. Isa. 59:1-2

If you have known sin in your life and continue to harbor
that sin, God will not hear your prayers. However, if you
confess your sins and keep short accounts with God, He will
hear your prayers.

What is the implication of verses like these? By not
listening when we are praying, God is essentially punishing
us, judging our sin by choosing not to hear. This raises a very
important point. How can God judge a child whom He has
already forgiven? Heb. 10:17 says very clearly, *Their sins and
iniquities will I remember no more.* To answer the question we
must remember the distinction between our spirit and soul.

The day we were saved from sin and given eternal life, our
spirit was made completely righteous (2 Cor. 5:21). Nothing
can change that. Positionally and legally, God never remem-
bers our sins any more; they are under the blood of Calvary.
We are His children, which means that on the level or plane of
our spirit, we can never be judged for our sins — past,
present, or future — for our spirit is righteous. Nevertheless,
our soul continues to sin, and when we do so, we break
fellowship with Him. It is like a child who offends his or her
parents through disobedience. The misbehavior does not
terminate the legal parent/child relationship. But it does
result in judgment — punishment for the child. In like
manner, God does indeed judge the sins of His children on the
soul level, and one of the ways He judges is by not hearing
our prayers.

## 2. God removes His hand of spiritual blessing from those saints who continue in sin.

> He that covereth his sins shall not prosper: but whoso confesseth and forsaketh them shall have mercy. Prov. 28:13

Notice the implication of this verse. The Lord does not show mercy to those saints who conceal their sins and refuse to confess and forsake them. He deals in judgment, not mercy.

Furthermore, from Psalm 1 we learn that God's hand of spiritual blessing is upon the righteous — those who live uprightly, without continued sin in their lives — but He judges those who walk in sinfulness. Clearly, these are references to the soul plane and not the spirit plane.

## 3. God does not forgive the sins of those saints who refuse to forgive others.

> For if ye forgive men their trespasses, your heavenly Father will also forgive you: But if ye forgive not men their trespasses, neither will your Father forgive your trespasses. Matt. 6:14-15

Wait a minute! How can God not forgive the sins of saints when we are told plainly, *Their sins and iniquities will I remember no more*, Heb. 10:17? Again, we must think on two planes, not merely one. On the spirit-salvation plane we are forgiven, but on the soul-sanctification plane we are not forgiven if we do not forgive others. Thus, we are eternally secure, even if we don't forgive others, but we face God's judgment, both here and now and at the Judgment Seat, if we refuse to forgive.

## 4. God does not show mercy or forgiveness to those saints who do not fear Him.

> 1 Bless the Lord, O my soul: and all that is within me, bless his holy name.
> 2 Bless the Lord, O my soul, and forget not all his benefits:
> 3 Who forgiveth all thine iniquities; who healeth all thy diseases;
> 4 Who redeemeth thy life from destruction; who crowneth thee with lovingkindness and tender mercies;
> 8 The Lord is merciful and gracious, slow to anger, and plenteous in mercy.

9 He will not always chide: neither will he keep his anger for ever.

10 He hath not dealt with us after our sins; nor rewarded us according to our iniquities.

11 For as the heaven is high above the earth, so great is his mercy toward them that fear him.

12 As far as the east is from the west, so far hath he removed our transgressions from us.

13 Like as a father pitieth his children, so the Lord pitieth them that fear him.

17 But the mercy of the Lord is from everlasting to everlasting upon them that fear him, and his righteousness unto children's children;

18 To such as keep his covenant, and to those that remember his commandments to do them.

Ps. 103:1-4, 8-13, 17-18

Many have made the mistake of taking v. 12 out of context, claiming it is referring to the initial salvation of our spirit. But the context does not bear that out. Look carefully at the preceding verse (v. 11) and the succeeding verse (v. 13), and in fact, several places in the psalm. Virtually the entire chapter is about God bestowing His mercy and forgiving those that *fear Him*. This is obviously a sanctification passage, not a justification passage. These verses apply to the saving of the soul.

Now consider the implication. If God bestows His mercy and forgiveness upon those who fear Him, then what is the converse? He does not bestow His mercy and forgiveness upon those who do not fear Him. Which means that v. 12 is not a promise to all saints, but only those saints who fear Him, those who obey His commandments (v. 18).

Interestingly, the psalmist clarifies that God forgiving and forgetting and bestowing His mercy is, according to v. 2, a benefit. The word *benefits* is defined as recompense, or reward. One way that God rewards those who fear Him is by forgiving and forgetting. In fact, v. 4, He "crowns" them with His loving-kindness and tender mercies. Furthermore, according to v. 17, His reward of mercy and forgiveness is eternal!

Consider one shocking conclusion of this passage. If God forgives and forgets all the transgressions of those who fear Him, and if He does so eternally, as a reward, then what does that mean for those saints who do not fear him? As a very minimum, it means God does not forget their transgressions in this life or at the Judgment Seat. Which means, of course, they will receive a negative reward at the Bema.

Incidentally, what does it mean to fear God? Fearing God involves four things:

1. Having a tremendous awe or reverence for Him
2. Dreading the thought of displeasing Him
3. Hating sin as He hates it
4. Submitting self to Christ

We must understand that the consequences for not fearing God are dire. No mercy or forgiveness now (on the soul level); no mercy or forgiveness then (again, on the soul level).

## 5. God "condemns" those saints who walk after the flesh rather than the Spirit.

> There is therefore now no condemnation to them which are in Christ Jesus, who walk not after the flesh, but after the Spirit. Rom. 8:1

Of course, this verse begs the question: What about those saints who are walking in the flesh? Apparently, there is condemnation for them. "Wait a minute!" someone might interject, "Are you suggesting some Christians may go to Hell?" Of course not! For whatever reason, many Christians have been trained to think of condemnation exclusively as Hell. However, the word in the Greek simply means a negative verdict — presumably, both now and at the Judgment Seat. In fact, the verb form of the word is used several times in the New Testament in reference to saints, as in the following verse:

> Grudge not one against another, brethren, lest ye be condemned: behold, the judge standeth before the door. James 5:9

Yes, even Christians can be condemned, in the sense that they can be judged and punished. Ultimately, they can be given a negative verdict at the Bema if they persist in sinful, fleshly living.

From chapter six of Romans onward, the apostle Paul has been addressing matters of sanctification, not justification. Rom. 8:1 is set in that sanctification context. For years I made the mistake of ending the verse after the words, *Christ Jesus*. I essentially ignored the second half of the verse, perhaps because my hermeneutical grid couldn't explain how it fit. But I now realize the importance of the remainder of the verse. It makes the sentence conditional. There is no condemnation — no negative verdict now or at the Judgment Seat — for those who are in Christ *and* who are walking in the Spirit as opposed to the flesh.

To suggest the verse is referring to salvation (i.e., justification) is to take the position that in chapter seven Paul is describing his struggle to become a Christian. That is not correct. Paul, in chapter seven, is describing his struggle as a believer to get victory over sin. He could not get victory of his own self-effort, but once he depended on Christ, he appropriated the victory. In that context, Rom. 8:1 is saying there will not be a negative verdict for those saints who walk in the Spirit, the life of victory.

Walking is the idea of taking reiterated steps. Thus, we have action in this verse, behavioral action. So we dare not relegate this to justification. Clearly, this is progressive sanctification. To be sure, there is no condemnation to believers in a salvation sense either, for we are eternally secure, but that is not the point of this particular verse.

Now, consider the implication. If there is no negative verdict for those who are walking in the Spirit, then what about those who are walking after the flesh? We must conclude there is a negative verdict for them.

Someone may interject, "The Bible says our *works* will be judged at the Bema, not our sins." Indeed, our works will be made manifest (1 Cor. 3:13-15), but does not the Bible speak of evil works, or works of the flesh, as well as spiritual works?

> For we must all appear before the judgment seat of Christ; that every one may receive the things done in his body, according to that he hath done, whether it be good or bad. 2 Cor. 5:10

The word *bad* at the end of this verse means "evil." In fact, it is most often translated *evil* throughout the New Testament

— several dozen times. Believers will be judged, not only for the good works, but for the evil works, which are unconfessed sins. They are called *works of the flesh*.

> Now the works of the flesh are manifest, which are these; Adultery, fornication, uncleanness, lasciviousness, Idolatry, witchcraft, hatred, variance, emulations, wrath, strife, seditions, heresies, Envyings, murders, drunkenness, revellings, and such like: of the which I tell you before, as I have also told you in time past, that they which do such things shall not inherit the kingdom of God. Gal. 5:19-20

These are not one-time sins. It's not as if one mess-up and you're out of the kingdom. No, thankfully, the verb *do* — in the phrase, *they which **do** such things* — is *prasso* (Gr.) and means "to practice or perform repeatedly" (per Strong), implying the continual doing of these things. God plainly labels continued sinning as *works* of the flesh, and the apostle warns that continuing in the *works* of the flesh (continued sinning) will result in disinheritance from the kingdom. Yes, we will be judged for our *works* — both spiritual works as well as works of the flesh.

Please understand, I am not suggesting that God keeps a detailed ledger of every sin you commit with plans to replay it for you on some type of heavenly big-screen television. That is highly unlikely. His focus does not seem to be on individual sins, per se. Rather, he is looking to see if continued sinning has kept you from fellowship with Jesus and going all the way in discipleship. If your soul is not saved at the Judgment Seat, it will not merely be for the lack of good works. It will also be for the copious sinning in which you continued, never seeking forgiveness.

## 6. God sometimes takes the life of those saints who sin.

> For the time is come that judgment must begin at the house of God: and if it first begin at us, what shall the end be of them that obey not the gospel of God? And if the righteous scarcely be saved where shall the ungodly and the sinner appear? 1 Pet. 4:17-18

God's judgment begins at His house, with His people. What does He judge? He judges our service for Him and also our motivations — the thoughts and intents of the heart. But if we look back at the Scriptures we get a good glimpse at what God judges. He primarily judges sin!

In Exod. 32 God's redeemed people, who had been saved by the blood at the Passover, made a golden calf in direct disobedience to the second commandment. God would have killed the people, but Moses interceded and God judged by sending a plague instead. Then Jehovah showed Moses His glory while making this proclamation:

> And the Lord passed by before him, and proclaimed, The Lord, The Lord God, merciful and gracious, longsuffering, and abundant in goodness and truth, Keeping mercy for thousands, forgiving iniquity and transgression and sin, and that will by no means clear the guilty; Exod. 34:6-7

Yes, God forgives sin, but only for those who confess their sin. He does not clear the guilty. Think of Nadab and Abihu, the sons of Aaron, priests who chose to offer incense improperly, in defiance of God's instructions. God killed them. He judged their sin.

In Num. 14 the people of Israel listened to the discouraging, evil report of the ten spies who did not believe God about taking possession of the Promised Land. As a result, the nation rejected God's will and sinned through their unbelief. Moses pleaded with God to spare them, for God was about to kill them all. In fact, Moses quoted what God had said to him back in Exod. 34.

> The Lord is longsuffering, and of great mercy, forgiving iniquity and transgression, and by no means clearing the guilty ... Pardon, I beseech thee, the iniquity of this people according unto the greatness of thy mercy ... And the Lord said, I have pardoned according to thy word: But as truly as I live ... all those men which have seen my glory, and my miracles, which I did in Egypt and in the wilderness, and have tempted me now these ten times, and have not hearkened to my voice; Surely they shall not see the land which I sware unto their fathers, neither shall any of them that provoked me see it. Num. 14:18-23

What was the problem with the wilderness generation? Was it merely motivation? No, it was blatant behavioral sin. They repeatedly refused to believe God. They tested Him ten times, and did not hearken to His voice. What was the consequence of their sin? God killed the ten spies and consigned the remainder of that generation to wander and die in the wilderness. They were never able to enter the Promised Land, because of the sin of unbelief. The faithful spies, Caleb and Joshua, on the other hand, were exempted from the punishment and rewarded abundantly.

King Saul was judged by God for refusing to kill all the Amalekites, as God had instructed. He lost his kingdom and died in battle because of the sin of disobedience. King David was judged by God for the sin of adultery with Bathsheba and murdering Uriah the Hittite.

Granted, these are Old Testament examples, but we serve the same God in the New Testament era, and He describes Himself as a consuming fire (Deut. 4:24; Heb. 12:29). Examples can also be given from the early church.

Ananias and Sapphira were judged for lying to the Holy Spirit. God instantly killed both of them. Though God doesn't typically judge so swiftly and severely, He can if He so desires. In 1 Cor. 5 Paul admonished the church to discipline a member who was living incestuously. The church was not to tolerate his sin; rather, they were, *To deliver such an one unto Satan for the destruction of the flesh, that the spirit may be saved in the day of the Lord Jesus,* 1 Cor. 5:5. If the man did not repent, then Satan would destroy his soul. Yes, he would be *saved,* but it would be *so as by* (through) *fire.*

In 1 Cor. 11 some who had partaken of the Lord's Supper unworthily were sickly and others had died because of God's judgment upon them. Every one of these instances of God's judgment was due to specific sin.

Thankfully, God disciplines His children, according to Heb. 12, to purge us from the sins in our life that keep us from fellowshipping with Him. The purpose of discipline is purging, to produce in us the peaceable fruit of righteousness. This implies that God often disciplines us when we are not living in righteousness; when we are living in sin. Some might argue that God's present judging in our lives is not the same as His discipline. But 1 Cor. 11:32 says, *When we are judged, we are chastened of the Lord.* In other words, God's present judgment, in the sense of punishment, is one form of chastening, with the intent of purging us of sins, so He can present us as a chaste virgin at His judgment bar (2 Cor. 11:2).

If God judges us *now* for sin, why would He not do so at the Judgment Seat? The point is that He *will* do so, for those sins that remain unconfessed; sins in which we persist, presumptuous sins. Perhaps that is why the psalmist cried out:

> Keep back thy servant also from presumptuous sins; let them not have dominion over me: then shall I be upright, and I shall be innocent from the great transgression. Ps. 19:13

However, we must make an important clarification. While God's present judging is for purging purposes, His future Judgment at the Bema, when negative verdicts are issued, is punitive. The purpose of the outer darkness, to be discussed in Chapter 10, is punitive, not purgatory.

## 7. God does not continually cleanse those saints who walk in darkness.

> 6 If we say that we have fellowship with him, and walk in darkness, we lie, and do not the truth:
> 7 But if we walk in the light, as he is in the light, we have fellowship one with another, and the blood of Jesus Christ his Son cleanseth us from all sin.
> 8 If we say that we have no sin, we deceive ourselves, and the truth is not in us.
> 9 If we confess our sins, he is faithful and just to forgive us our sins, and to cleanse us from all unrighteousness.
> 1 John 1:6-9

What does it mean to walk in the light? According to v. 6, it is the opposite of walking in darkness. To walk in darkness is to sin, to walk in the flesh. In fact, God gives an example of walking in darkness in 1 John 2:11 — hating your Christian brother. Walking in the light, then, is *not* sinning, for it is walking in the Spirit.

Consider the powerful truth of v. 7. When we are walking in the light, not sinning, the blood of Christ is continually cleansing us from all sin. That being the case, what does this suggest when we are walking in darkness? The blood of Christ is not continually cleansing us from sin. How can this be for a blood-bought saint? It is obviously speaking on the soul plane. On the spirit plane, you are completely righteous. The blood of Christ has cleansed you completely, and you are eternally secure. But the soul plane is up to you and affects rewards at the Judgment Seat.

## 8. God offers no more sacrifice for sins for those saints who continue in willful sin.

> For if we sin wilfully after that we have received the knowledge of the truth, there remaineth no more sacrifice for sins, But a certain fearful looking for of judgment and fiery indignation, which shall devour the adversaries. Heb. 10:26-27

What a frightening prospect! It is the expectation of no more sacrifice for sins for those who continue in willful, persistent sin. To whom does this refer?

Those of an Arminian theological persuasion interpret this to mean Christians who persist in heinous sin can lose their salvation. Another view is held by some from the Calvinist theological tradition, who believe this admonition refers to so-called, professing Christians that have demonstrated by their lifestyle they were never saved in the first place. I believe both of these theological positions are incorrect biblically. However, the Arminian position appears to be closer to the truth than the Calvinist position. For the Arminian sees something as being lost, and he is right about that. But to suggest salvation is what is lost is a doctrinal error. How can that which is eternal be lost? The Bible very clearly teaches the doctrine of eternal security. Those who are saved have passed from death unto life. That transaction happened at a point in time in the past and can never be lost or forfeited. Once saved, always saved. You, dear child of God, have been credited with the righteousness of Christ in your spirit, and you have been sealed with the Holy Spirit of God.

How, then, do we understand what is being lost, according to this verse? The key is to remember the scriptural concept of two salvations (spirit v. soul — see Chapter 2) and then to determine in every scripture passage which salvation is in focus. Is it the salvation of the spirit, resulting in instantaneous justification and positional sanctification — that is, salvation from eternal condemnation? Or is it salvation of the soul, resulting in progressive sanctification over one's lifetime and positive reward at the Judgment Seat? Unfortunately, many Bible students fail to distinguish between the two and assume all references to salvation in the New Testament refer to salvation of the spirit, that is, salvation by grace through faith alone. Thus, they assume the phrase *saving of the soul* at the end of this passage is soteriological.

> But we are not of them who draw back unto perdition; but of them that believe to the saving of the soul. Heb. 10:39

But as we have seen, it is not hermeneutically accurate to insist that *the saving of the soul* is referring to justification. As we already learned in Chapter 2, our soul is saved (i.e., sanctified) only to the extent we cooperate with God's working in our lives. There is the prospect of a believer's soul not being saved (i.e., sanctified) in this life because of foolish, carnal choices to live for self. When that believer stands before Jesus at the Judgment Seat, his soul will be forfeited in the sense that any positive reward will be lost and only negative reward will be given. Instead of hearing, *Well done, good and faithful servant,* that believer will hear, *Thou wicked and slothful servant.* And so this passage is not speaking of lost people and their need for justification. It is warning saved people of their need for sanctification, so that their soul can be deemed "saved" at the Judgment Seat.

Notice what happens for those who have no more sacrifice for sins. God judges, perhaps here and now, but certainly then. The fiery testing furnace at Christ's Bema will devour their soul, just as it did the body and soul of those who died under the Mosaic law without mercy. The judgment will be even greater for New Testament saints.

> Of how much sorer punishment, suppose ye, shall he be thought worthy, who hath trodden under foot the Son of God, and hath counted the blood of the covenant, wherewith he was sanctified, an unholy thing, and hath done despite unto the Spirit of grace? Heb. 10:29

Christians that continue in willful sin will be punished — yes, *punished!* — for essentially trampling Christ under foot. They have discounted the blood of Christ and insulted the

Holy Spirit, and for that they will be punished more severely than the Old Testament Israelites who defied the Mosaic law.

How do we know this is addressed to the saints? Verse 26 specifically says they received the knowledge of the truth, and knowledge in this verse is not merely the Greek word *gnosis*, or basic knowledge. It's *epignosis* — full, experiential knowledge. At the very least, this implies saving knowledge. But the word implies so much more. There is no doubt that this person has been saved, justified, and positionally sanctified (per v. 29) and has learned much about the Christian life.

How can we know when salvation references are justification-oriented vs. sanctification-oriented? Here is a clue to interpreting salvation passages in the New Testament. Typically, when salvation is mentioned as in the *past* tense, it is referring to salvation from eternal condemnation, or the salvation of the *spirit*. But when salvation is mentioned as in the *future*, it is referring to the salvation of the *soul*, discipleship that leads to rewards.

In the extreme case of someone who lives willfully, carnally, and selfishly (however God judges that), there remains no more sacrifice for sins. We must understand this statement in reference to the plane-of-the-soul and the matter of rewards, not as a reference to the plane-of-the-spirit and the matter of eternal security.

Thus, we can conclude, based on Scripture, that unconfessed sins (at least in a general sense) will be judged by Jesus at the Judgment Seat. Why is it so important to understand this truth? If this were not the case, consider the ramifications. Believers would tend to live licentiously. Incidentally, those within traditional dispensationalism who teach all saints will essentially be rewarded in some degree at the Judgment Seat and live happily-ever-after, are unwittingly promoting licentious behavior. For if there are no serious consequences at the Judgment Seat, if there is no prospect of negative reward, what would be the incentive for believers to become overcomers by the grace of God? We will discuss motivations more extensively in Chapter 11.

# Chapter 8

---

# Looking for a City

In this chapter and the next, we will explore the two realms of the kingdom. Let's begin with the ruling realm of the kingdom, which is the heavenly city of reward.

> For he looked for a city which hath foundations, whose builder and maker is God. Heb. 11:10

For what was Abraham looking? We know he was not looking merely for Canaan, for Abraham actually made it to that Promised Land after leaving Ur and Haran. He lived there and saw it. So Canaan is not the city for which he was looking.

> These all died in faith, not having received the promises, but having seen them afar off, and were persuaded of them, and embraced them, and confessed that they were strangers and pilgrims on the earth. Heb. 11:13

The common conclusion from these verses is that Abraham was looking for Heaven. But that is not entirely correct either. Abraham and others in the Old Testament were not merely looking for the eternal state. Rather, they were looking for a city of reward, a place not on this earth, but a place closely connected with this earth, as we shall see. That is why

Abraham lived in tents with Isaac and Jacob, the heirs with him of the same promise (Heb. 11:9). That is why they lived as strangers and pilgrims on Earth — because they didn't see *this earth* as their home; they saw *that city* as their home. They were *persuaded* of the coming reward. They *embraced* it by faith. They *professed* that they were merely strangers and pilgrims on Earth. In other words, their lifestyle was entirely focused on the age to come, not the present age. The same is said of Moses.

> Esteeming the reproach of Christ greater riches than the treasures in Egypt: for he had respect unto the recompence of the reward. By faith he forsook Egypt, not fearing the wrath of the king: for he endured, as seeing him who is invisible. Heb. 11:26-27

Moses endured by fixing his eyes of faith on the invisible God. He had respect unto the recompense of the reward. The verb *had respect* in the Greek is the idea of looking away from all else and focusing intently on the one main thing. The phrase *recompense of reward* is one Greek word and means "requital." Of course, requital is something given in return. Whether positive or negative reward, it is what the person earns. In other words, these patriarchs of Israel were not focused on the here and now; they were focused on a coming city. Indeed, they were focused on a city of reward — a city connected with requital or payout. It consumed their attention, for they wanted to qualify for that city of reward. Incidentally, the city of reward is only for the faithful, so these patriarchs sought to qualify for it; they looked away from everything else and gazed intently upon the prize. That is one way we know this is not referring to the gift of eternal life. God's gift of eternal life is by grace through faith alone. There is no work involved for eternal life. But the city of reward is based entirely on one's spiritual work for Christ.

Where is this city? It seems to be suspended above the earth, but visible to those on Earth, during the millennial kingdom. Then it will also be seen in connection with the new Heaven and new Earth in the eternal state. But it is an actual, special city of reward that hovers over Earth.

Now if that sounds far-fetched, just wait. I will demonstrate the point from the Scriptures, and I believe if we will connect the dots that God has given to us in His Word, the conclusion will be marvelous to comprehend! Indeed, I believe this is largely what God was speaking of when giving us the promise:

> But as it is written, Eye hath not seen, nor ear heard, neither have entered into the heart of man, the things which God hath prepared for them that love him. 1 Cor. 2:9

Notice the verse does not say, "The things which God has prepared for those who are *saved*." It says, "for those that *love* Him." It is a spectacular reward for faithfulness. In fact, the verse is a quote from an Old Testament Messianic kingdom prophecy, Isa. 64:4, which is followed by a verse that specifies the need to qualify:

> Thou meetest him that rejoiceth and worketh righteousness, those that remember thee in thy ways. Isa. 64:5

The city of reward is not for all saints. It is for those faithful saints whose works are righteous.

## Five Evidences of the city of reward

### 1. Jacob's dream

> And he dreamed, and behold a ladder set up on the earth, and the top of it reached to heaven: and behold the angels of God ascending and descending on it. Gen. 28:12

Abraham looked for the city of reward and although, presumably, he never saw it with physical eyes, he did view it with the spiritual eyes of faith. But Jacob is a different story. Do not jump to the conclusion that Jacob saw the third heaven, the place of God's dwelling. This word *heaven* is translated from the same Hebrew word as used in the Genesis creation account.

> In the beginning God created the heaven and the earth. Gen. 1:1

> And God called the firmament heaven. Gen. 1:8

The word *heaven* can refer to the sky, and that is how it is being used here in this verse. What does Jacob see? I would suggest he sees the city of reward, and I think that will become clearer as we go along. Specifically, he sees a *ladder* — that is, a staircase — ascending from Earth to this place in the sky. And he sees the angels (messengers) of God ascending and descending on it. Notice it does not say the angels are descending and ascending, which would be more the order we might expect. I believe the order is significant, and we will see why in a moment.

Why does God allow Jacob to have this dream? We must remember the context. Jacob has fled from home as a fugitive from his brother. Though Jacob has some spiritual weaknesses that God will work on throughout the next few decades of Jacob's life, he is also a deeply spiritual man. He is focused on receiving the status of firstborn son — though he was the younger son — and receiving the blessing. Jacob knew God had promised this to his parents, and he went after it, perhaps not in the best way, but he wanted it nonetheless, whereas Esau spurned it. That will factor into the end of our study in this chapter. Jacob is now running away from home, with his parents' blessing, in order to escape the wrath of Esau and to find a wife from his extended family rather than amongst the ungodly Canaanites.

God takes this opportunity to confer upon Jacob the patriarchal promises that had been made to his father Isaac and grandfather Abraham. (See Gen. 28:13-15). How encouraging! God promises His presence to Jacob and the fulfillment of the Messianic promises, saying, *In thy seed shall all the families of the earth be blessed.* That is a Messianic promise and a direct reference, not only to the Messianic sacrifice, but ultimately to the Messianic kingdom. Every nation will be blessed by that kingdom. So our first evidence testifying to the city of reward is Jacob's dream.

## 2. Christ's encouragement to Nathanael

Jesus saw Nathanael coming to him, and saith of him, Behold an Israelite indeed, in whom is no guile! Nathanael saith unto him, Whence knowest thou me? Jesus answered and said unto him, Before that Philip called thee, when thou wast under the fig tree, I saw thee. Nathanael answered and saith unto him, Rabbi, thou art the Son of God; thou art the King of Israel. Jesus answered and said unto him, Because I said unto thee, I saw thee under the fig tree, believest thou? thou shalt see greater things than these. And he saith unto him, Verily, verily, I say unto you, Hereafter ye shall see heaven open, and the angels of God ascending and descending upon the Son of man. John 1:47-51

Why does Jesus make this promise to Nathanael? I believe there are two reasons. First, I think it is because of Nathanael's declaration, *Thou art the Son of God; thou art the King of Israel.* Nathanael instantly recognizes Jesus as the Messiah. The second reason is because of Jesus' proclamation about Nathanael, *Behold an Israelite indeed, in whom is no guile!* How often do we read Jesus making a proclamation of this nature in the Gospels? Hardly ever! I believe Jesus is saying this man is qualified for ruling with Christ in His Messianic kingdom. Then Jesus tells Nathanael what his eye has not seen, nor his ear heard, neither has entered into his heart — the things Jesus has prepared for him!

Hereafter ye shall see heaven open, and the angels of God ascending and descending upon the Son of man. John 1:51

Remarkably, Jesus uses a different word for *see* than we might expect. It is not the normal word for viewing something with the eyes. This word *see* means "to gaze with wide open eyes, as at something remarkable" (Strong). This is a New Testament reference to the very thing Jacob had seen in the Old Testament — the city of reward in the coming Messianic kingdom, the place where saints who are faithful will rule and reign with Christ.

Again, notice the angels are ascending and descending on the stairway to Heaven, not the other way around. Why is this? I believe these angels are not the heavenly beings created by God to do His bidding. I believe they are "angels" in the general sense of messengers. In this context, I believe they are faithful saints who will rule from the heavenly city of reward over the earth in the coming kingdom. If that is the case, then the reason for ascending, then descending, is because these messengers originate on Earth, not in Heaven. In my opinion, these are the faithful saints who will ascend up into the heavenly city of reward, where they will dwell, and that will be their headquarters for ruling over the earth. They will periodically descend to Earth with instructions for those living on Earth, and that will include those who are saved but deemed unfaithful to live in the city of reward.

Notice on whom the faithful saints will ascend and descend — on the Son of Man, for He is the ultimate ruler, the King. The faithful saints will operate on His authority. He will "beam them up" to Heaven, so to speak, and then back down again to Earth to do His bidding. I suspect this is not an actual staircase, as we know it, but some heavenly means of transportation to/from Earth. The third evidence of the city of reward is …

## 3. The unique term used by Jesus to describe it

Much ink has been used by commentators to describe the difference between the terms *kingdom of heaven* and *kingdom of God*. I tend to think they are generally synonymous terms and that both of them refer to the millennial kingdom, which Jesus then turns over to the Father at the end of the thousand years to become the eternal kingdom. Why, then, does Jesus frequently use the term *kingdom of heaven*?

We must remember that Matthew wrote his gospel to a Jewish audience, and his purpose was to emphasize Christ's position as Messianic King. All the Jews were expecting Messiah to establish a kingdom on Earth. That had been prophesied in the Old Testament repeatedly. Furthermore, they all understood it to be a kingdom of God. We could debate whether that means sent by God or a kingdom actually ruled by God, but that is not important to our present discussion. What is important is that the Jewish people were expecting a literal, Messianic kingdom of God on Earth. Numerous Old Testament passages make that clear, but it is outside the scope of this book to explore those passages.

Why, then, the use of the term *kingdom of heaven*? Because, I believe, it emphasizes a certain realm of the Messianic kingdom that Jesus was offering to the Jews — the kingdom of heaven. Unfortunately, the full meaning of the term does not come out in the English translation. Most literally, this phrase from the Greek translates, "the kingdom of the heavens." That is abundantly clear in the original and implies that it is not merely a kingdom sent *from* the heavens. It is a kingdom of the heavens, located *in* the heavens, but closely connected with Earth, as the ladder in Jacob's dream and Jesus' conversation with Nathanael suggests.

Now I said earlier the Jews were expecting a literal, earthly Messianic kingdom, and the phrase *kingdom of God* would have conveyed that Jewish understanding. An earthly Messianic kingdom was indeed coming. But what the Jews of Jesus' day apparently did not understand was that there was a second aspect to the Messianic kingdom — the city of reward component, or we could call it the heavenly component, the kingdom of the heavens.

Imagine an earthly Messianic kingdom with a heavenly city as headquarters. That city will apparently hover over the earth and be connected to the earth, at least in the sense that faithful citizens who dwell in the heavenly realm will have access back and forth. Presumably, those who dwell on Earth will not have access to the heavenly realm. I will illustrate that in a moment.

Think of it! Jesus uses a special term and Matthew records it in his gospel to the Jews — describing one realm of the kingdom of God — the heavenly realm, where the faithful saints will dwell and rule together with Christ. It is the castle, so to speak, the city of reward, and it is somehow suspended above Earth. To enter that realm of the Messianic kingdom, one has to qualify by faithful service for Christ, and that includes obedience. All other saved people who have not lived in obedience and have not borne fruit will automatically enter the earthy realm of the kingdom and dwell there. But there is a vast difference between the two realms, as we shall see. You don't want to settle for the earthly kingdom!

Whenever we see the term *kingdom of God*, I think we should conclude that it is referring to the entire Messianic kingdom — both the earthly realm and the heavenly realm. Whenever we see the term *kingdom of heaven*, meaning "kingdom of the heavens," I think we should conclude that it is referring solely to the heavenly realm of the Messianic kingdom. That understanding helps to explain why two terms are repeatedly used in the gospels. By the way, when Jesus uses the term, *enter into the kingdom*, He is not talking about getting saved from eternal condemnation. He is talking about qualifying to enter into the city of reward, the heavenly realm of the Messianic kingdom. We will explore this concept in more detail in a future book, God willing. We come now to our fourth evidence of this city of reward.

### 4. The warnings in the book of Hebrews not to squander our heavenly reward

In essence, the warnings in the book of Hebrews caution believers about forfeiting an inheritance in the city of reward. We read earlier of Moses in Heb. 11, who *had respect unto the recompense of reward*. That is, he made decisions to leave the glories of Egypt and instead to suffer with the Israelites because he was determined to turn aside from all else and focus on the recompense, the payout of rewards. Like Abraham, he was looking for a city with foundations, whose builder and maker is God. He was focused on the heavenly realm of the kingdom.

Is this something with which we need to be concerned? Absolutely, the book of Hebrews is probably the most grossly misinterpreted book of the Bible. But when understood from an inheritance/reward perspective, it makes perfect sense. The book of Hebrews is not about persevering unto salvation (that is, eternal life). The salvation mentioned in Hebrews is not soteriological, referring to justification. It is referring to the sanctification aspect of salvation, or soul-salvation. Thus, the book is written to believers and focuses on persevering unto reward. At least five warnings are given, urging saints to persevere in their walk with the Lord, or else they could forfeit their inheritance.

The showcase illustration referred to repeatedly in the book is that of Israel wandering in the wilderness. It is discussed extensively in chapters 3-4. Israel was saved at the Exodus and went out into the wilderness as redeemed people. But they hardened their hearts against Moses and the Lord and rebelled. They became carnal and unbelieving, culminating at Kadesh-Barnea in the ultimate apostasy of not entering the Promised Land. As a result, God consigned them to wander in the wilderness, where they died. They never inherited the Promised Land, except for two faithful men and their families. The writer of Hebrews, on that basis, warns all saints to beware of the prospect of losing our reward and not inheriting the Promised Land — both now and in the coming kingdom.

We go now to Heb. 12, which is the climax of the warnings. In 12:18-21 we are told that our inheritance is not Mt. Sinai, which was terrifying. Rather, starting in v. 22, our inheritance is Mt. Zion, which is magnificent and glorious.

> 22 But ye are come unto mount Sion, and unto the city of the living God, the heavenly Jerusalem, and to an innumerable company of angels,
> 23 To the general assembly and church of the firstborn, which are written in heaven, and to God the Judge of all, and to the spirits of just men made perfect,
> 24 And to Jesus the mediator of the new covenant.
> Heb. 12:22-24

Abraham was looking for a heavenly city, and so are we. It is called *heavenly Jerusalem* — a city with foundations, whose architect is God. Notice how it is described in v. 23. In this heavenly Jerusalem, which I would contend is the city of reward, there will be both faithful Jews and faithful Gentiles. That is why it is called a general assembly. And it seems to include angels, per v. 22. But notice the additional description in v. 23: *To the church of the firstborn.* What is a church? It is a called-out assembly. Jesus is firstborn; He earned that title following His death, burial, resurrection and ascension. Furthermore, He wants us to earn that title. It's not automatic. According to Rom. 8:29, Jesus wants to be the firstborn among many brethren. All saints are children of God (heirs), but not all saints are firstborn sons (joint-heirs with Christ). The latter is an inheritance status that is conferred and results in reigning with Christ in the heavenly portion of his kingdom. Here it is described as a city, heavenly Jerusalem, a called out assembly of firstborn saints, which are written in Heaven. Yes, their names are in the book of life as saints, but further, their names are check-marked, so to speak, as qualifying saints, having earned the privilege of ruling with Christ.

Notice also in v. 23, *the spirits of just men made perfect.* *Perfection* is not a justification term; it is a sanctification term. It is the idea of going all the way in discipleship — complete maturity in sanctification. So here is how I understand the last phrase of v. 23. The heavenly city of reward — heavenly Jerusalem — will be populated by those who are called out from among all saints at the Judgment Seat, for they are deemed worthy of the status of firstborn son, a double inheritance, granting them the right to live in the heavenly Jerusalem and rule with Christ. They are the ones who are perfected in their sanctification process. Are you one of those? Now the warning.

> See that ye refuse not him that speaketh. For if they escaped not who refused him that spake on earth, much more shall not we escape, if we turn away from him that speaketh from heaven: Wherefore we receiving a kingdom which cannot be moved, let us have grace, whereby we may serve God acceptably with reverence and godly fear: For our God is a consuming fire. Heb. 12:25, 28-29

Do you get the point? You will not be part of the city of reward unless you qualify. So beware of disqualifying yourself! We come now to the fifth evidence of the city of reward.

## 5. The book of Revelation clearly describes it

> 1 And I saw a new heaven and a new earth: for the first heaven and the first earth were passed away; and there was no more sea.
> 2 And I John saw the holy city, new Jerusalem, coming down from God out of heaven, prepared as a bride adorned for her husband.
> 3 And I heard a great voice out of heaven saying, Behold, the tabernacle of God is with men, and he will dwell with them, and they shall be his people, and God himself shall be with them, and be their God.
> 4 And God shall wipe away all tears from their eyes; and there shall be no more death, neither sorrow, nor crying, neither shall there be any more pain: for the former things are passed away.
> 5 And he that sat upon the throne said, Behold, I make all things new. Rev. 21:1-5

The verses that follow (21:9-22:5) seem to give a greater description of the city of reward. Notice in v. 1 above that John sees a *new* Heaven and a *new* Earth and, in v. 2, a *new* Jerusalem. Since each of these three places is new, would it not imply that there is a former Heaven and a former Earth and a former Jerusalem coming down from God out of Heaven? Indeed. In fact, it seems the first Jerusalem comes down from Heaven in vs. 9-10:

> And there came unto me one of the seven angels which had the seven vials full of the seven last plagues, and talked with me, saying, Come hither, I will shew thee the bride, the Lamb's wife. And he carried me away in the spirit to a great and high mountain, and shewed me that great city, the holy Jerusalem, descending out of heaven from God. Rev. 21:9-10

This, I believe, occurs at the beginning of the millennium and is the heavenly Jerusalem, the place we have referred to as the city of reward. It will hover over the earth and be connected by a stairway of sorts. Faithful saints will dwell there and rule with Christ from that place in the heavens. At the end of the millennium it appears the heavenly Jerusalem will ascend away from the existing Heaven and Earth and then descend again later to hover over the new Earth for eternity.

Though it is outside the scope of this book, the description of this city is magnificent. I would encourage you to read Rev. 21:9-22:5 and revel in *the things which God hath prepared for them that love Him,* 1 Cor. 2:9. This is truly a marvelous city of reward. Incidentally, v. 19 speaks of the *foundations* of the wall of the city. What was Abraham looking for? A city with *foundations,* whose builder and maker (architect) is God. I believe this very city of reward that will hover over Earth in the millennium and during the eternal state is what Abraham was looking for — and we should be looking for it too! Are you looking for the city of reward? It is the kingdom of the heavens, the heavenly Jerusalem.

To conclude this chapter, we return to Heb. 12.

> Wherefore we receiving a kingdom which cannot be moved, let us have grace, whereby we may serve God acceptably with reverence and godly fear: For our God is a consuming fire. Heb. 12:28-29

We are admonished, *Let us have grace.* In other words, don't spurn God's grace; accept it; embrace it; and thereby live the Christ-life of victory. If you do, you will inherit the heavenly city of reward; but if not, you will be like Esau.

Follow peace with all men, and holiness, without which no man shall see the Lord: Looking diligently lest any man fail of the grace of God; lest any root of bitterness springing up trouble you, and thereby many be defiled; Lest there be any fornicator, or profane person, as Esau, who for one morsel of meat sold his birthright. For ye know how that afterward, when he would have inherited the blessing, he was rejected: for he found no place of repentance, though he sought it carefully with tears. Heb. 12:14-17

What a dreadful end to Esau's life. He forfeited his inheritance as firstborn son and lost the blessing too. Don't let Esau characterize your end.

# Chapter 9

# Prepare to Be the Bride

A white wedding dress is traditionally associated with purity. When a bride who has been unfaithful, immoral, impure, wears a white wedding dress, she is misrepresenting herself; her action is hypocritical. The outward clothing, in that case, does not represent the true, inward person. The image that is being conveyed is inconsistent with the actual life, and it is repulsive to those who know the real person. Imagine how Christ must feel when His children are unfaithful, immoral, impure in their spiritual relationship to Him, and yet they try to cover over their stained, dirty garments with a clean, white garment — a facade — as if to cloak the underlying problem. Just as audacious to the Savior is when His unfaithful children assume they will receive white robes of righteousness one day and become His chaste bride. However, as the passage below indicates, the clean, fine linen garments are only given to those who have made themselves ready to be the wife of Christ, only to those saints who have prepared to meet the groom.

> 7 Let us be glad and rejoice, and give honour to him: for the marriage of the Lamb is come, and his wife hath made herself ready.
> 8 And to her was granted that she should be arrayed in fine linen, clean and white: for the fine linen is the righteousness of saints.

9 And he saith unto me, Write, Blessed are they which are called unto the marriage supper of the Lamb. And he saith unto me, These are the true sayings of God. Rev. 19:7-9

## White Robes of Righteousness

As we will demonstrate in this chapter, when you meet Jesus at the Judgment Seat, you will receive a white garment only to the extent that He deems you worthy. Furthermore, a white garment of righteousness is the proper attire for the wedding festivities. Those who are not granted white garments at the Judgment Seat will not attend the wedding festivities. Thus, I ask you an important question: Will you be at the Marriage Supper of the Lamb? "Oh yes," you may reply, "I am a child of God; I have been clothed with the righteousness of Christ."

The temptation is to think we automatically possess such garments because of our position in Christ, as righteous ones, justified in our spirit. However — and this is critically important to understand — the pure, untainted garments granted to the saints here in v. 8 are not based on our position, that is, Christ's righteousness. What does the end of the verse say? The garment is granted contingent on the righteousness of saints. Indeed, the garment *is* the righteousness of saints. In fact, in the Greek, the word *righteousness* is actually plural. The fine linen is the "righteousnesses (plural) of the saints" — or, we could say, the righteous acts of saints. The acts are righteous because they have been imparted by Jesus, as He lives His life through the saints. Clearly, from the grammar one must conclude that white robes are awarded based on the righteous behavior of individual saints.

What does this mean? This means the garment is not based on imputed righteousness (justification in the realm of the spirit), but rather on imparted righteousness (progressive sanctification in the realm of the soul). May I put it bluntly? Your lifestyle choices here and now are determining the type of garment you will be given at the Judgment Seat.

Thou hast a few names even in Sardis which have not defiled their garments; and they shall walk with me in white: for they are worthy. He that overcometh, the same shall be clothed in white raiment. Rev. 3:4-5a

Clean, white, pure linen garments will only be granted to those who live righteously, those who are deemed overcomers. If you choose to live for yourself, unfaithful to Christ, you will not receive righteous garments. Unlike modern day brides, you will not be able to fool anyone — and certainly not Jesus — by putting on a false garment. Your works will be made manifest at the Judgment Seat. Your true colors will be revealed, and a garment will be appointed to you based on who you really are. If your garment is not pure and white, you will not participate in the Marriage Supper of the Lamb. While the imputation of Christ's righteousness provides eternal security, it does not ensure your inclusion at the Marriage Supper. That is a humbling thought. If you do not get ready, you will not qualify to be His bride and will not participate in the wedding festivities that launch the millennial kingdom.

## Qualifying as Bride

I believe the Scriptures teach the bride of Christ is not comprised of the entire church but only a subset of the church that Jesus, the bridegroom, deems faithful and worthy to be His bride. The king will not have an impure, unfaithful wife to rule at His side as queen. Qualifying to be the bride of Christ is equivalent to qualifying as a first-born son and qualifying to be a co-heir with Christ. They are all synonymous terms, and they all relate to ruling and reigning with Christ, not to eternal security.

Some may object that Paul's discussion of husbands and wives in the book of Ephesians is a picture of Christ and His church, namely, that all saints will be sanctified, cleansed, and presented as glorious. But that is not what Paul is teaching.

Husbands, love your wives, even as Christ also loved the church, and gave himself for it; That he might sanctify and cleanse it with the washing of water by the word, That he might present it to himself a glorious church, not having spot, or wrinkle, or any such thing; but that it should be holy and without blemish. Eph. 5:25-27

Notice that Christ desires to present the church to Himself as spotless, holy, and unblemished — that He *might* sanctify and cleanse it; that He *might* present it a glorious church —

but it is by no means guaranteed. It is His intent, but it will only happen to the extent the saints live pure, untainted lives. He never forces anyone to obey Him. Incidentally, in the context, the cleansing with washing of water is practical, not positional, for the means of washing is the Word, not the blood. A biblical marriage — involving a husband loving his wife with a purifying, cleansing love and a wife submitting to her husband — is a beautiful picture of this. However, how many Christian marriages are less than biblical in the way they operate? In like manner, multitudes of saints are not prepared to be the bride of Christ. They are less than biblical in behavior and have thereby excluded themselves from co-rulership with Jesus.

The parallel passage in Colossians also demonstrates that presentation of saints as chaste is conditional.

> And you, that were sometime alienated and enemies in your mind by wicked works, yet now hath he reconciled In the body of his flesh through death, to present you holy and unblameable and unreproveable in his sight: If ye continue in the faith grounded and settled. Col. 1:21-23

Christ wants to present the saints as *holy and unblameable.* But this does not happen automatically. It is conditional — *If ye continue in the faith grounded and settled.* The point is that while imputed righteousness in one's spirit results in eternal security, it does not guarantee reward, which includes a bridal relationship with Christ. Reward is based on the righteous behavior of saints. Again, we see this in Paul's letter to the Corinthians:

> For I am jealous over you with godly jealousy: for I have espoused you to one husband, that I may present you as a chaste virgin to Christ. But I fear, lest by any means, as the serpent beguiled Eve through his subtilty, so your minds should be corrupted from the simplicity that is in Christ. 2 Cor. 11:2-3

Paul's intent was to be able to present the church at Corinth to Christ as a chaste (pure) virgin, a worthy bride. But it's not automatic; it's conditional, and that is evidenced by Paul's use of the word *may* in v. 2 — *that I **may** present you.* In v. 3 we find the prospect of believers not submitting to the sanctification process and therefore not being deemed worthy. Yet another conditional passage is found in Romans:

> Wherefore, my brethren, ye also are become dead to the law by the body of Christ; that ye should be married to another, even to him who is raised from the dead, that we should bring forth fruit unto God. Rom. 7:4

The first part of the verse is unconditional — *Ye also are become dead to the law by the body of Christ*. But the second part of the verse is conditional in terms of only being potential — *That ye should be married to another ... that we should bring forth fruit unto God*. This doesn't always happen. Christians do not yield themselves to the Lord and so do not become espoused to Christ — which is akin to abiding in Him — and therefore do not bear fruit.

## The Ten Virgins

We now turn our attention to the teaching of Christ, where we see this principle illustrated in parabolic form.

> Then shall the kingdom of heaven be likened unto ten virgins, which took their lamps, and went forth to meet the bridegroom. And five of them were wise, and five were foolish. Matt. 25:1-2

Parables are metaphors that use everyday situations to illustrate spiritual truths. In this case, Jesus uses the concept of Jewish virgins getting ready for marriage in their culture to get across the utter importance of being ready to be His bride.

We must not read our western cultural traditions regarding marriage into the passage. Rather, we must interpret according to the marriage customs prevalent during Bible times. Following is a brief overview of the five aspects of marriage during the New Testament era (adapted from ISBE and other sources):

1. **Betrothal.** The bridegroom-to-be would meet with the father of the bride-to-be and agree to marry his daughter. The result, if they could come to an agreement, was a legally binding marriage transaction. The couple was considered married at that point, but they would live apart for a year or

so while the bride prepared for the wedding and the groom prepared the home.

2. **Processional**. At the conclusion of the waiting period, the bride would be transferred from her father's house to the house of her new husband. This would typically happen at night in a torch-lit procession, involving guests. The bride would not know what night the groom would appear, so she had to be prepared for his arrival. A town crier of sorts would come by a little in advance to warn the bride of the groom's arrival.

3. **Festivities**. Sometimes, an entire week of feasting and celebrating with friends would precede the wedding ceremony.

4. **Ceremony**. The actual wedding observance would be held toward the end of the week of celebration.

5. **Marriage Supper**. A large concluding supper would be held at the end of the celebration, after which the groom and his bride would be ushered off to their home to start their lives.

It is important to keep this custom in mind when studying the parable, for it was vivid in the psyche of the Jewish audience Jesus was addressing.

The moral of this story is simple: those who are faithful and ready (i.e., spiritually prepared) to meet Christ will be allowed to participate in the wedding festivities that inaugurate the millennium, to be held in the heavenly city of reward. Those who are unfaithful will be excluded from the celebrations. This does not mean they are unbelievers; rather, they are believers who have not lived righteously. They are *saved; yet so as by fire*, 1 Cor. 3:15. Accordingly, they do not qualify to rule and reign with Jesus in the heavenly realm of His kingdom.

The necessary preparation for attending the wedding festivities is a proper wedding garment. As we have already seen, Rev. 19:8 specifies a garment of *fine linen, clean and white* granted to wedding participants, which *is the righteousness of saints*.

Some would have us believe the parable of the virgins is referring to saved and unsaved. The five ready virgins are those who are saved, they say, and the five unprepared virgins are those who are unsaved. However, despite the popularity of that interpretation, it is not consistent with the text, as we shall see.

First, the whole group is comprised of ten. The number ten appears to be the number of completion in the Scriptures, and so in this case would be a reference to the entire church, comprised entirely of saved people. Second, all ten women in the parable are virgins. The natural man is never compared to a virgin, which is a picture of positional righteousness and purity. That imagery would be inappropriate for unbelievers, who are dead in trespasses and sins and enemies of God. Furthermore, the apostle Paul said in 2 Cor. 11:2, *I have espoused you to one husband, that I may present you as a chaste virgin to Christ.* He was speaking to saints at the church of Corinth, not to the lost. His intent was to be able to present them as chaste (pure) virgins, a prospect which is possible for believers because of our position in Christ. However, presentation as a pure virgin at the Judgment Seat is not a given, for it is conditional, based on one's lifestyle.

Some insist this kingdom parable refers to the Jews rather than the church. That is unlikely, for in Matt. 21:43 Jesus had pronounced that the kingdom would be taken from the Jewish nation and given to a "nation" bringing forth the fruits of the kingdom. We understand that "nation" to be the church of Jesus Christ. If that is correct, then in this parable Jesus is illustrating the necessity of qualifying to enter the ruling realm of the coming kingdom.

> They that were foolish took their lamps, and took no oil with them: But the wise took oil in their vessels with their lamps. While the bridegroom tarried, they all slumbered and slept. And at midnight there was a cry made, Behold, the bridegroom cometh; go ye out to meet him. Then all those virgins arose, and trimmed their lamps. And the foolish said unto the wise, Give us of your oil; for our lamps are gone out. But the wise answered, saying, Not so; lest there be not enough for us and you: but go ye rather to them that sell, and buy for yourselves. And while they went to buy, the bridegroom came; and they that were ready went in with him to the marriage: and the door was shut. Matt. 25:3-10

**Ready for the Groom's Arrival**

The storyline is simple. The ten virgins are preparing for the coming of the bridegroom, but according to the marriage customs outlined earlier, they don't know when that will be. Since the bridegroom will come at night, they have lamps, filled with oil, and the wise virgins have vessels of surplus oil besides. The foolish virgins do not have the extra oil. Oil in the Scriptures is typically a picture of the Holy Spirit. Another indication that these virgins are all saved is that they all have oil in their lamps, representing the indwelling presence of the Holy Spirit. Those who have surplus oil, we could say, not only have the Spirit's indwelling, they also are filled with the Spirit. They are walking in the Spirit, living the Christ-life as faithful disciples of Jesus.

The wise virgins are like Christians who have renounced the self-life and have let go of worldly pleasures. They are regularly appropriating God's grace by faith to let Jesus live His life through them. They are fruit-bearing, victorious Christians. In contrast, the unfaithful are living for them-selves, captivated by the world, indifferent to the Lord's return, not walking in the Spirit.

Since the hour is late, all of these virgins go to sleep. Soon they are awakened by the crier at midnight, who says, *Behold, the bridegroom cometh; go ye out to meet him.* Notice the emphasis on readiness to meet the bridegroom — in our case, readiness to meet Jesus at the Judgment Seat.

They all get up and trim their lamps to meet the bridegroom, which is very likely indicative of Christ's returning to gather up His saints. A picture of the Judgment Seat follows, for while five of the virgins are faithful, being filled with the Spirit and therefore ready to meet the bride-groom, the other five are unfaithful, not being filled with the Spirit and therefore not ready to meet the bridegroom.

In the parable, the unprepared virgins don't have enough oil, so they must go and buy some for themselves. The wise virgins cannot give any of their own, since every person will stand before Christ, accountable only for him or her self. Spirit-filling is a personal thing and cannot be shared with others. Every man (or woman in this case) must be filled, independent of others. The wise virgins are wise because they have been living for Jesus; the foolish virgins are foolish because they have been living for self.

While the foolish virgins are off trying to obtain more oil for their lamps, the bridegroom comes. The wise virgins enter the wedding banquet hall, and the door is shut. The unprepared miss their opportunity to attend the marriage and related festivities.

Incidentally, what door is shut? Is it the door to Heaven? Absolutely not! Jesus is not talking about eternal life. He is talking about the coming kingdom, in particular, the marriage of Christ and His church that inaugurates the millennium. In like manner, unfaithful Christians are excluded from the marriage festivities, indicating disinheritance from the kingdom of the heavens, the ruling realm of the Messianic kingdom. They are given no opportunity to rule and reign with Jesus. What will happen to them? We will discuss that in the next chapter.

Think of it! Jesus will be the King of the kingdom, and His bride will be the queen, so to speak. The queen will rule and reign with the King in His kingdom. That is why the unfaithful church is not included in the marriage festivities or the marriage itself — because they will not be ruling as Christ's bride (His queen) in the kingdom.

## "I Know You Not"

What becomes of the five foolish virgins (or we could say the unfaithful Christians)?

> Afterward came also the other virgins, saying, Lord, Lord, open to us. But he answered and said, Verily I say unto you, I know you not. Matt. 25:11-12

The statement of Christ, *I know you not*, tends to confuse some into thinking these virgins cannot possibly represent Christians. However, a brief explanation of the Greek wording used can clear up any potential misunderstanding.

Jesus is omniscient, and obviously knows everybody, so His statement *I know you not* cannot refer to intelligent comprehension. He is using the term relative to the context. The

Greek word translated *know* in v. 12 is the idea of *intimate* knowledge. Vine says Christ's statement suggests, "You stand in no relation to me." That doesn't mean they are lost and condemned. Relative to the parable and the context, it means they are not fit to be His bride. They are not closely related to Jesus, because of their unrighteous lifestyle that has resulted in broken fellowship. Thus, they are not allowed entrance to the wedding festivities and the marriage, for they do not qualify to enter the banquet hall.

It is as if Jesus is saying, "You five foolish, unfaithful virgins are not worthy to be my bride; my relationship to you is not close. You will not rule and reign in my kingdom as my queen." Immediately following Christ's pronouncement — *I know you not* — He admonishes His disciples:

> Watch therefore, for ye know neither the day nor the hour wherein the Son of man cometh. Matt. 25:13

Many Christians assume that *all* believers will inherit the coming kingdom, *all* will rule and reign with Christ in some degree, *all* will inherit the promises for overcomers, *all* will live happily-ever-after, and *all* will live without sorrow in the millennium. But it seems that such theology is not only inconsistent with the Scriptures, but also contributes unwittingly to licentious behavior.

It is important that we not be ashamed at His coming (1 John 2:28) and that we lose not our reward (2 John 8). Thankfully, every child of God can earn robes of righteousness, because every saint has been given the provision of Christ's righteousness. If you are appropriating His grace by faith (Rom. 5:2) to perform His will on Earth, then you are a candidate for the wedding garment. It is high time that saints prepare to be the bride!

# Chapter 10

# Saints in Outer Darkness

The door is shut on the five unprepared virgins in Christ's parable of the virgins (Matt. 25:1-13). As we saw in the previous chapter, they represent unfaithful Christians who are unprepared to meet Jesus at the Judgment Seat. They will be left outside the ruling realm of Christ's kingdom, the heavenly city of reward. Where, then, do they go? To answer this important question, we need to investigate the three passages that use the term *outer darkness*.

## Children of the Kingdom in Outer Darkness

> And when Jesus was entered into Capernaum, there came unto him a centurion, beseeching him, And saying, Lord, my servant lieth at home sick of the palsy, grievously tormented. And Jesus saith unto him, I will come and heal him. The centurion answered and said, Lord, I am not worthy that thou shouldest come under my roof: but speak the word only, and my servant shall be healed. For I am a man under authority, having soldiers under me: and I say to this man, Go, and he goeth; and to another, Come, and he cometh; and to my servant, Do this, and he doeth it. When Jesus heard it, he marvelled, and said to them that followed, Verily I say unto you, I have not found so great faith, no, not in Israel. Matt. 8:5-10

The centurion in this narrative is obviously Roman, a Gentile. Jesus is amazed at this man's simple faith, his dependence on Jesus to heal a servant back home. Even though the centurion is a man of great authority and power he, nonetheless, makes no demands on Jesus, unlike the Jews, who were essentially demanding inclusion in the heavenly realm of the kingdom (*We have Abraham to our father*, Matt. 3:9). Notice what Jesus says about the self-righteous Jews:

> And I say unto you, That many shall come from the east and west, and shall sit down with Abraham, and Isaac, and Jacob, in the kingdom of heaven. But the children of the kingdom shall be cast out into outer darkness: there shall be weeping and gnashing of teeth. Matt. 8:11-12

In context, the many coming *from the east and west* are Gentiles, and *the children of the kingdom* are Jews. They are children of the kingdom in the sense that the Messianic kingdom is for them, the covenant people of God, according to the Old Testament prophets. Nothing can change that. Indeed, Israel will one day be in the earthly millennial kingdom. But the Jewish nation, by rejecting Christ's offer of kingdom inheritance and rulership, will not be allowed entrance into the heavenly realm of the kingdom, the city of reward. Instead, the nation, generally speaking, will be in the darkness outside — that is, in the earthly realm of the kingdom, not in the Messiah's direct presence. Of course, any faithful Jews will inherit the heavenly Jerusalem, and that is evidenced by the presence of Abraham, Isaac, and Jacob in the kingdom of the heavens. The same is true of Christians of any era of church history.

To interpret *outer darkness* as Hell is to suggest that the Jews, the children of the kingdom, will go to the lake of fire. But that is inconsistent with the term *children of the kingdom*, and the context of this passage, as well as the Old Testament prophecies. Some may question the *weeping and gnashing of teeth*, but that is simply an oriental way of expressing shame and regret on behalf of those saints who could have qualified for the heavenly kingdom, but squandered their inheritance, like Esau. They will sorrow over their lost opportunity. If only the nation had believed the message of John the Baptist and

Jesus and repented of their sins and found national healing! If only they had gotten right with God! If only Christians would live for Jesus rather than self!

We turn our attention now to two parables of Jesus, both found in Matthew's gospel.

## Parable of the Improper Wedding Garment

1 And Jesus answered and spake unto them again by parables, and said,

2 The kingdom of heaven is like unto a certain king, which made a marriage for his son,

3 And sent forth his servants to call them that were bidden to the wedding: and they would not come.

4 Again, he sent forth other servants, saying, Tell them which are bidden, Behold, I have prepared my dinner: my oxen and my fatlings are killed, and all things are ready: come unto the marriage.

5 But they made light of it, and went their ways, one to his farm, another to his merchandise:

6 And the remnant took his servants, and entreated them spitefully, and slew them.

7 But when the king heard thereof, he was wroth: and he sent forth his armies, and destroyed those murderers, and burned up their city.

8 Then saith he to his servants, The wedding is ready, but they which were bidden were not worthy.

9 Go ye therefore into the highways, and as many as ye shall find, bid to the marriage.

10 So those servants went out into the highways, and gathered together all as many as they found, both bad and good: and the wedding was furnished with guests.

11 And when the king came in to see the guests, he saw there a man which had not on a wedding garment:

12 And he saith unto him, Friend, how camest thou in hither not having a wedding garment? And he was speechless.

13 Then said the king to the servants, Bind him hand and foot, and take him away, and cast him into outer darkness; there shall be weeping and gnashing of teeth.

14 For many are called, but few are chosen.

Matt. 22:1-14

The parable begins by comparing the kingdom of the heavens (the heavenly city of reward) to a king (God the Father), who prepares for his son's marriage (Jesus uniting with His bride, His faithful co-regent). From the parallel text in Luke 14:16-24 we learn this wedding is, more specifically, the wedding supper, or feast, which precedes the actual wedding. It is equated with the Marriage Supper of the Lamb in Rev. 19:7-9, which inaugurates the millennial kingdom.

Virtually all commentators identify the King as God the Father and His Son as Jesus Christ. In vs. 1-6 the servants that bid folks to come to the wedding are likely the Old Testament prophets and perhaps John the Baptist. Those who are bidden to the wedding by the King's servants are the Jewish people. They will not come (v. 3), and actually make light of the invitation and ignore it (v. 5). In fact, the bidden (religious leaders) persecute and kill the prophets and John the Baptist (v. 6). This may also be referring to Jesus and to the twelve apostles, who are persecuted and martyred.

How does the King respond to this treatment of his servants? The King, in His anger, sends forth His armies, destroying the murderers and burning up their city. Most conservative commentators see this as the destruction of Jerusalem in AD 70. The King insists on moving ahead with the wedding, as everything has been meticulously and beautifully planned. So He sends His servants out again (v. 8). This time, the servants (very likely the apostles) are instructed to go outside the city (Jerusalem) into the highways and hedges (the realm of the heathen), compelling all those who will come, both bad (Gentiles) and good (Jews) — v. 10.

The wedding is finally filled with those who respond to the king's invitation. What about the man who comes to the wedding but is not properly attired? His offense is that he is not wearing an appropriate wedding garment. This out-of-place man suggests a real rubbing point, not merely for the King but for all who would correctly interpret the passage.

Some say the wedding garments refer to both the imputed righteousness of Christ and the imparted righteousness of the saints. They would argue that saved people live and act like it, and thus the impartation of robes of righteousness must, of necessity, accompany any persevering saint. Those who have not persevered in righteousness are not true saints and will not stand before Christ at the Judgment Seat, much less be present at the Marriage Supper, they would claim.

But is that what Jesus is saying in this parable? This man's presence before the King demonstrates that he has accepted the King's invitation. Furthermore, the King refers to him as *friend*. When the King asks the man why he is not wearing the wedding garment, the man is speechless, literally muzzled. He can say nothing; he has no adequate response, for he knows better. This is not a lost man, waking up to the fact that he doesn't belong in Heaven. This is a saved man, waking up to the reality that he is not worthy to be part of the bride.

I believe this scene is reminiscent of the Judgment Seat of Christ, when some are *saved, yet so as by* (through) *fire*, and will undoubtedly have nothing to say for themselves. This passage implies that only those saints who are deemed worthy, based on their obedience — their righteous behavior, as determined by Christ at the Judgment Seat — will be allowed entrance to the Marriage Supper of the Lamb and, presumably, to the heavenly realm of the Messianic kingdom which is inaugurated by the Marriage. All saints, it seems, are not granted automatic entrance into the city of reward.

## Bound Hand and Foot

Some tend to discount this view of the parable because they interpret what happens to the improperly dressed wedding guest as being cast into Hell. But does the Bible say he is cast into Hell? Look at v. 13. Let us discuss these phrases one-by-one. First, *bind him hand and foot*. We must remember, this is a parable, a metaphor. The binding is not literal; it represents something. In the context of an unfaithful Christian who does not inherit the city of reward, the binding of hand and foot would indicate a loss of freedoms. This saint will not be able to move about as freely in the millennial world; he will not be able to participate in activities of significance. He will not be able to make an impact in the kingdom, for he will be constrained in his opportunities.

Think for a moment of all the rebellious Christians who chafe at restrictions on their so-called freedoms. They don't like rules; they don't want to be told what to do. By resisting their authorities — be it Dad and Mom, or the policeman, or the teacher, or their employer, or whoever — they are responding in defiance and rebellion toward their God-ordained authorities. It will not go well for those folks at the Judgment Seat. The irony is that the very thing they resist so much in life — restrictions on their freedom — will be the very thing they endure throughout the coming kingdom age — much more severe restrictions on their so-called freedoms. Oh, the importance of submitting to our authorities here and now, for it is ultimately submitting to God. Those believers that have submissive hearts — who are willing to give up their perceived rights in order to honor their authorities — will be rewarded with freedoms in the kingdom. So the first recompense here is loss of freedom.

## Taken Away

Second, *Take him away and cast him into outer darkness*. The word *cast* sounds violent to us. But it need not be. The same Greek word is used in Matt. 9:38, where Jesus tells us, *Pray ye therefore the Lord of the harvest, that he will send forth* (cast out) *labourers into his harvest*. To *cast out* does not necessarily imply violence. In Mark 1:43, after Jesus healed the leper, *He straightly charged him, and forthwith sent him away*. The phrase *sent him away* is the same Greek word, meaning to cast out. The word *cast* is simply the idea of thrusting forth; it need not have a negative connotation.

This man is sent to outer darkness. His offense is not wearing a proper wedding garment. He is not worthy to be at the wedding festivities. As we noted above, the term does not refer to Hell. It is critical to understand that the term *outer darkness* simply means "the darkness outside." These marriage feasts would typically be held at night, so that one put outside would be in relative darkness compared with the brightness of the banquet hall. But we must remember: this is a parable; it is a metaphor. The darkness outside is likely referring to the earthly realm of the kingdom in contradistinction to the bright and glorious heavenly ruling realm.

Here is a Christian who so longs to be at the marriage festivities with the bridegroom, for it is beautiful, and it is full of blessing. But he does not qualify to be there; he is sent outside. Like a foolish virgin, he hears those words from the lips of Jesus: "I know you not. I don't have an intimate relationship with you. You don't qualify to be at my wedding." The imagery used implies that he longs to be inside the bright and beautiful banquet hall rather than outside in comparative darkness. Furthermore, he longs for freedom, rather than being restricted in his activities. How does he respond to the loss of inheritance? As v. 14 says, with *weeping and gnashing of teeth*. He sorrows and agonizes over his foolishness, consciously regretting it; he is full of remorse and grief. While that *could* describe the emotional state of one in Hell, could it not also describe the emotional state of one who has been excluded from the glories of the kingdom?

If some true believers, based on Christ's determination at the Bema, are excluded from the Marriage Supper, because their life is not worthy of receiving a righteous wedding garment, will they not weep and consciously regret being put out? Notice v. 14: *Many are called, but few are chosen.* In the context this seems to mean that many are saved, but few of the saved will be deemed worthy of ruling and reigning with Christ in His kingdom. That is a sobering thought.

Let us move now to a brief review of one more parable, found in Matt. 25.

## Parable of the Talents

> For the kingdom of heaven is as a man travelling into a far country, who called his own servants, and delivered unto them his goods. And unto one he gave five talents, to another two, and to another one; to every man according to his several ability; and straightway took his journey. Matt. 25:14-15

Again, Jesus uses a metaphor to illustrate His point. In this case, He likens Himself to a master or lord who is about to travel a far distance and will be gone for some time. He entrusts to His servants a great responsibility. Before getting too far, I need to point out that all three are called *servants*, even though one fails in his responsibility. Some commentators suggest the third servant is, in reality, a non-servant, merely a professing servant. They need this third servant to be cast into Hell in order to interpret this parable according to their theological system. But that is reading into the passage.

The third man is called a *servant* like the other two servants. The words of Jesus should settle the matter for us.

To servant number one, the master gives five talents, a unit of money. To servant number two, he gives two talents, and to servant number three, he gives one talent. The implication is they are to use their resources responsibly during the master's absence. The Master is obviously Jesus, who is gone away during this church age, but will one day hold His saints accountable (at the Judgment Seat) for their actions while He is gone. When the master returns, He requires an accounting of His servants.

> After a long time the lord of those servants cometh, and reckoneth with them. And so he that had received five talents came and brought other five talents, saying, Lord, thou deliveredst unto me five talents: behold, I have gained beside them five talents more. His lord said unto him, Well done, thou good and faithful servant: thou hast been faithful over a few things, I will make thee ruler over many things: enter thou into the joy of thy lord. He also that had received two talents came and said, Lord, thou deliveredst unto me two talents: behold, I have gained two other talents beside them. Matt. 25:19-22

Servant number one now has ten talents. Servant number two has four talents. In both cases, they have been responsible in their use of the Master's resources, and now have twice as much to show for their labors. The Master is pleased! He says this to each of them, individually:

> Well done, good and faithful servant; thou hast been faithful over a few things, I will make thee ruler over many things: enter thou into the joy of thy lord. Matt. 25:23

This has nothing at all to do with salvation or Heaven. It has to do with the kingdom, and Jesus makes that clear at the start of the parable. For their faithfulness, these two servants become inheritors of the city of reward. The Master makes them *ruler over many things.* Because they have lived faithfully and responsibly in their small realm of influence on Earth, Jesus rewards them with big responsibilities in the world to come. What a glorious prospect! But then we see the unfaithful servant.

Then he which had received the one talent came and said, Lord, I knew thee that thou art an hard man, reaping where thou hast not sown, and gathering where thou hast not strawed: And I was afraid, and went and hid thy talent in the earth: lo, there thou hast that is thine. His lord answered and said unto him, Thou wicked and slothful servant, thou knewest that I reap where I sowed not, and gather where I have not strawed: Thou oughtest therefore to have put my money to the exchangers, and then at my coming I should have received mine own with usury. Take therefore the talent from him, and give it unto him which hath ten talents. For unto every one that hath shall be given, and he shall have abundance: but from him that hath not shall be taken away even that which he hath. Matt. 25:24-29

The unfaithful servant makes excuses for himself and actually blames the Master for his irresponsible, unfaithful behavior. He returns nothing to the Master. He hides the talent that had been entrusted to Him. As a result, his portion is taken away and given to the faithful servant. This is the equivalent of being put out of the banqueting hall, bound hand and foot. His second punishment is found in the last verse of the parable:

And cast ye the unprofitable servant into outer darkness: there shall be weeping and gnashing of teeth. Matt. 25:30

Once again we encounter outer darkness, but it is not Hell as is so frequently misinterpreted. It is the darkness outside. It is exclusion from inheriting the heavenly city of reward. The unfaithful servant is left outside the castle of the king, so to speak. And you will be too, dear Christian, if you do not live faithfully and obediently to Jesus, using the resources He has given to you, the provision of "Christ in you."

## Distinguished From the Parable of the Pounds

Incidentally, it is important to mention that the parable of the pounds in Luke 19:12-27 is very similar to this parable, with a couple of key exceptions. In the parable of the pounds, there are ten servants. Ten, again, is the number of completion which, we believe, is a reference to the entire church. Each servant receives one pound. Why do they all receive the same amount? I believe the parable of the pounds is referring to the equal *provision* that all saints have in Christ. We all have the Holy Spirit; we all have Christ living within. He will determine one day, as part of our reward or punishment, the extent to which we appropriated His provision in this life. Those who did will be rewarded to some degree. Those who did not will be recompensed accordingly. Their pound will be taken and given to others.

In contrast, in the parable of the talents each person receives a different amount. I believe that demonstrates the different talents, abilities, circumstances, and opportunities in every Christian's life. We are all so different from one another in that respect. Thus, Jesus will judge us — not compared to others — but according to His expectations for us. Remember, He handsomely rewards both the servant who doubles his five talents and the servant who doubles his two talents. The point is that we all have the provision of Christ in our spirit — His righteousness living within us. So we have within the enabling power to obey and be faithful, if we will depend on Christ.

> That the righteousness of the law might be fulfilled in us who walk not after the flesh but after the Spirit. Rom. 8:4

Nevertheless, we all have different talents, abilities and opportunities for service. We were all saved at a different stage of life. So Jesus, the perfect Judge, determines according to both — our equal provision and our individual situation, which is God-given and customized to every individual. The all-important question of this chapter is this: At the Judgment Seat, will your reward be, *Well done, good and faithful servant,* or *Bind him hand and foot and take him away and thrust him into the darkness outside?*

In conclusion, we can now see that outer darkness is the negative counterpart to the positive city of reward. If the city of reward is the heavenly realm of the kingdom, outer darkness is likely the earthly realm. If the city of reward is inside the castle, so to speak, then outer darkness is outside the castle. If the city of reward is bright because of Jesus and all the glorified saints that are glowing there in some degree, then outer darkness is dark, relatively speaking, for the saints there are not glowing and Jesus Himself is not manifestly

SAINTS IN OUTER DARKNESS | 111

present. In my opinion, outer darkness is not a description of Hell, as is commonly taught. It is a description of the earthly realm of the Messianic kingdom. Many saints will be there, both Jews and Gentiles, and they will be ashamed, for having missed the opportunity to rule and reign with Jesus.

## Christian Purgatory?

Some are troubled by the concept of outer darkness. They view it as a sort of "Christian purgatory." However, there are major differences between the Roman Catholic doctrine of purgatory and the biblical doctrine of outer darkness, as distinguished in the following table:

| Outer Darkness | Purgatory |
|---|---|
| For those believers whose works are evil and not worthy of reward | For those whose works aren't good enough to get them to Heaven |
| Purpose: punitive reward | Purpose: purging of sins |
| Means: conscious regret and loss of some freedoms | Means: suffering that may include flames |
| Place: a realm of Christ's kingdom outside the New Jerusalem, possibly on Earth | Place: intermediate state between Heaven and Hell, possibly in the earth |
| Goal: deter present misbehavior | Goal: graduation to Heaven |
| An end in itself | A means to an end |
| Eternal | Temporal |

Clearly, purgatory is based on the erroneous doctrine of works salvation and so must be rejected by born again believers as unbiblical. It is undoubtedly a perversion of the truth of Judgment Seat fire (1 Cor. 3:13-15; Matt. 3:11) and outer darkness. However, it is incumbent on the student of the Scriptures not to "throw out the baby with the bath water." To reject a biblical understanding of outer darkness because some have perverted it would be a tragedy indeed. Better to teach the doctrine as taught in the Scriptures. Of course, that is the purpose for this book and this chapter in particular.

Outer darkness has nothing to do with the gift of eternal life. It is the negative reward that eternally secure believers will receive if they do not progress in sanctification according to God's will. Unlike purgatory, outer darkness is not a period of purging for the expiation of (atonement for) one's sins, the intent being a promotion to Heaven. The doctrine of purgatory is works-salvation extended beyond this life, as if to give a second chance to those who weren't good enough during their Earth life. We condemn such thinking as unbiblical. On the contrary, outer darkness is punitive as opposed to purging. Apparently, there will be no prospect of the believer's status changing throughout eternity. *(See note on p. 63).* The believer in outer darkness will always be outside the brightness of Christ's ruling realm, albeit in a world much grander than the present. The prospect of dwelling in the darkness outside throughout eternity should be a sufficient warning to believers to focus on the eternal rather than the temporal.

### The Dwarfs are for the Dwarfs

C.S. Lewis, in my opinion, has given a pertinent illustration of the outer darkness in his final book in *The Chronicles of Narnia, The Last Battle*. The book speaks of an imposter (a picture of antichrist) who poses as Aslan (the lion who symbolizes Jesus), working to deceive many. The deception is eventually exposed, and results in a great battle between good and evil (reminiscent of the Battle of Armageddon). During the battle, a group of fighters — the dwarfs — refuse to take sides, sometimes opposing evil and sometimes opposing good. Nevertheless, they are Narnians, of Aslan's country (the equivalent of born-again believers). They repeatedly chant, "the dwarfs are for the dwarfs," adamantly refusing to be taken in by either side. In the end, when evil is finally defeated and destroyed, the dwarfs are not banished from Aslan's kingdom, but rather remain in an isolated, boxed-in realm of the kingdom that is dark (for them). Others can see the beauties and brightness of Aslan's kingdom, and can see the dwarfs plainly and clearly. But the dwarfs cannot see anyone outside their little realm. They are blind to the glories and wonders of the world around them. It is as if they are living in a box made of one-way glass. Those on the outside of the box can see into the box, but those inside the box (the dwarfs) cannot see out. In fact, it is so dark inside the box they can hardly see anything.

Lucy, one of the children whom Aslan has appointed as queen of Narnia (representing a faithful believer) has pity on the dwarfs and asks Aslan to do something about their pitiful condition. Aslan demonstrates to Lucy by way of an object lesson that nothing can be done for those who don't want help. He instantaneously creates a magnificent banquet-type meal, including many delicacies for the dwarfs to eat. They don't realize from whence the food has come, and after tasting it, they spurn it, complaining that it tastes like food lying around a stable — hay and old turnips and raw cabbage leaves. The wine, they claim, tastes like dirty water from a donkey's drinking trough. Furthermore, a fight erupts in their invisible "box," because every dwarf suspects his fellow dwarfs of having something better than himself.

Aslan turns to Lucy and says, "You see, they will not let us help them. They have chosen cunning instead of belief. Their prison is only in their own minds, yet they are in that prison; and so afraid of being taken in that they cannot be taken out. But come, children. I have other work to do."

The dwarfs and their dark, isolated realm of the kingdom seem a fitting metaphor for outer darkness. The one difference is that the dwarfs are unable to comprehend their condition as different from anyone or anything else around them, whereas believers in the outer darkness will weep and gnash their teeth, consciously regretting that they did not live for Jesus and His eternal kingdom. Nevertheless, those believers who live for themselves are essentially chanting in dwarf-like fashion, "we carnal Christians are for ourselves."

# Chapter 11

---

# The Last Shall Be First

Does a system of merit at the Judgment Seat trouble you? Does it sound too much like the works-*salvation* of some religious belief systems? If so, remember that salvation from eternal condemnation is not in question at the Judgment Seat. Though it is possible to lose one's soul and be negatively rewarded, the positionally righteous spirit of a believer is eternally secure, nonetheless. Thus, works-*salvation* is completely out of the question. Eternal life is not at issue at the Bema; eternal rewards are at stake (1 Cor. 3:13-15).

Perhaps, then, you are concerned that being rewarded for meritorious behavior after salvation smacks of works-*sanctification*. If the doctrine of rewards is taught incorrectly, it surely can. The problem with works-*sanctification* is twofold. First, expecting works to sanctify (i.e., keeping a list or doing certain things to become spiritual) is one of the aspects of legalism Paul condemns in the epistle to the Galatians. The apostle made it very clear that we are sanctified the same way we are saved — by faith, not by works!

> This only would I learn of you, Received ye the Spirit by the works of the law, or by the hearing of faith? Are ye so foolish? having begun in the Spirit, are ye now made perfect by the flesh? Gal. 3:2-3

Nevertheless, spiritual works are definitely an essential component of progressive sanctification. Indeed, we will be judged for our works (1 Cor. 3:13-15). When James wrote to the believers scattered abroad, he reminded, *Faith without works is dead*, James 2:20. Despite what some theologians have taught through the centuries, James 2:14-26 has absolutely nothing to do with salvation from eternal condemnation. It is all about soul-salvation, or we could say, progressive sanctification. The point of James' admonition is faith that truly sanctifies is never devoid of works. If it is, then it is not sanctifying faith. It is dead, lifeless sanctification. In short, that believer is not growing in grace.

Unfortunately, in some segments of Christianity works are viewed as the *cause* of progressive sanctification, whereas in reality, they are the *effect*. True spiritual works can only flow out of one whose life has been filled with the Holy Spirit. As we come to know and submit to Christ in greater measure, we grow spiritually and learn to abide in Him. The fruit of such a life in union with Christ is evidenced by spiritual graces and spiritual works (in contradistinction to fleshly works — see Gal. 5:16-24 — and flesh-dependent works — see 2 Cor. 3:5-6). We will address the process of spiritual growth in Chapter 12 and hopefully clarify the difference between works-sanctification and sanctified works.

The second problem with the works-sanctification mentality is that it obligates God to reward according to what man *does* in the name of Christ, without regard to what motivates the *doing*. In spite of the fact that works may be done in flesh-dependence, the worker expects a reward. This has led many believers to an entitlement mentality with respect to rewards, an expectation that God has a divine sense of duty to reward their labor and activity for Christ, as *they* define it. Is this not especially true of some traditional dispensationalists, whose theology leads them to believe all saved people are, by nature of their position in Christ, overcomers, and therefore expected to inherit the rewards for overcomers? Undoubtedly, many will be shocked one day to discover that position in Christ and/or busyness for Christ will not necessarily accrue to positive reward. God is not bound to reward all works done in the name of Christ, particularly not those done with a works-sanctification mindset (see Matt. 7:21-23).

Of course, that raises a very important question. If we are not to have an entitlement mentality about rewards, then are rewards even a valid motivation for serving God?

## Motivations for Faithful Service

In the Scriptures we find at least four motivations for serving Christ faithfully:

### 1. Duty

> I beseech you therefore, brethren, by the mercies of God, that ye present your bodies a living sacrifice, holy, acceptable unto God, which is your reasonable service. Rom. 12:1

> It is required in stewards, that a man be found faithful. 1 Cor. 4:2

It is only reasonable and logical that we should serve God with every ounce of our being, considering all he has done for us! We are God's stewards; therefore, we should be faithful in our service.

> Let us hear the conclusion of the whole matter: Fear God, and keep his commandments: for this is the whole duty of man. For God shall bring every work into judgment, with every secret thing, whether it be good, or whether it be evil. Eccles. 12:13-14

At the end of an unsatisfying life, trying all that the world had to offer, Solomon concluded that the only meaningful thing is to fear God and obey Him. Indeed, this is our duty. In fact, God will judge us as to whether we did our duty.

> But which of you, having a servant plowing or feeding cattle, will say unto him by and by, when he is come from the field, Go and sit down to meat? And will not rather say unto him, Make ready wherewith I may sup, and gird thyself, and serve me, till I have eaten and drunken; and afterward thou shalt eat and drink? Doth he thank that servant because he did the things that were commanded him? I trow not. So likewise ye, when ye shall have done all those things which are commanded you, say, We are

unprofitable servants: we have done that which was our duty to do. Luke 17:7-10

Good servants do their duty even if they are never thanked, and they have an attitude of unworthiness about being a servant. As believers, we should recognize our unworthiness to be servants of Christ, demonstrating faithfulness to Him in everything we do.

## 2. Fear

> For we must all appear before the judgment seat of Christ; that every one may receive the things done in his body, according to that he hath done, whether it be good or bad. Knowing therefore the terror of the Lord, we persuade men. 2 Cor. 5:10-11

> Wherefore we receiving a kingdom which cannot be moved, let us have grace, whereby we may serve God acceptably with reverence and godly fear: For our God is a consuming fire. Heb. 12:28-29

Believe it or not, the Word of God points to fear as a valid motivation for serving in faithfulness. This is not an unhealthy, anxious trembling kind of fear, but rather a profitable, reverent dread of displeasing God. In addition to the above verses, 1 Pet. 4:17 reminds us, *Judgment must begin at the house of God,* and 1 Cor. 11:31 admonishes that we should judge ourselves lest we be judged by God.

## 3. Love

*We love Him, because He first loved us,* 1 John 4:19, and when we truly love Him, we will keep His commandments, John 14:15. The love of Christ constrains us (it compels us) not to live for ourselves, but for Him who died for us, 2 Cor. 5:14. This should be our greatest motivation to obey and serve in faithfulness, but it is also closely connected with rewards, as we shall see. Taking this to the ultimate, Paul says something rather startling in the love chapter.

> Though I bestow all my goods to feed the poor, and though I give my body to be burned, and have not charity, it profiteth me nothing. 1 Cor. 13:3

You can give everything you possess to the poor — and even die as a martyr! — both of which have rewards attached therewith if done out of the right motivation (Luke 14:13-14; Rev. 20:4). But if you are not motivated by love when you give your possessions or your life, it profits you nothing. You will forfeit any reward! That is convicting.

## 4. Rewards - both positive and negative

Although we are to be motivated by duty, fear of displeasing the Lord, and ultimately love, rewards are also motivational, to provoke obedience and faithful service, while deterring misbehavior and neglect of duty. More importantly, the heart of Jesus is to bring many sons unto glory (Heb. 2:10), a faithful bride that can co-rule with Him in His kingdom. Thus, God has graciously designed a system of rewards for His children, though we are unworthy of His favor. Seeing that He has ordained that rewards be given for faithful service, as well as punishment for unfaithful service, we ought to live in a manner that makes us worthy of His rewards. Let us strive to be rewarded, for that glorifies our Lord.

> But without faith it is impossible to please him: for he that cometh to God must believe that he is, and that he is a rewarder of them that diligently seek him. Heb. 11:6

In the Scriptures we find numerous rewards as motivators. Following are just a few from the Beatitudes:

> Blessed are the poor in spirit: for theirs is the kingdom of heaven.
> Blessed are they that mourn: for they shall be comforted.
> Blessed are the meek: for they shall inherit the earth.
> Blessed are they which do hunger and thirst after righteousness: for they shall be filled.
> Blessed are the merciful: for they shall obtain mercy.
> Blessed are the pure in heart: for they shall see God.
> Blessed are the peacemakers: for they shall be called the children of God.
> Blessed are they which are persecuted for righteousness' sake: for theirs is the kingdom of heaven. Matt. 5:3-10

On-and-on we could go through the rest of the New Testament. The list is quite long and includes many of the parables. For instance, the faithful servants in the parable of the talents are handsomely rewarded.

> His lord said unto him, Well done, thou good and faithful servant: thou hast been faithful over a few things, I will make thee ruler over many things: enter thou into the joy of thy lord. Matt. 25:21

### The apostle Paul expressed his heartfelt desire for reward:

> Know ye not that they which run in a race run all, but one receiveth the prize? So run, that ye may obtain. And every man that striveth for the mastery is temperate in all things. Now they do it to obtain a corruptible crown; but we an incorruptible. 1 Cor. 9:24-25

> I press toward the mark for the prize of the high calling of God in Christ Jesus. Phil. 3:14

Is it selfish of Paul to want to be rewarded for serving God? No, it is biblical. In Matt. 19:27 Peter asks Jesus what the disciples will receive for forsaking all and following Him. Jesus never rebukes Peter for selfishness but promises him and the others a magnificent reward. Then He promises a great reward to anyone who will do the same, and that includes all of us. Clearly, we are given motivations to serve, even as we are expected to serve. God even warns us not to lose our reward:

> Look to yourselves, that we lose not those things which we have wrought, but that we receive a full reward. 2 John 8

Consider this very important question. Shouldn't we be doing all of these things, whether we are rewarded or not? Shouldn't we be poor in spirit and mournful and meek and hungering and thirsting after righteousness and merciful, etc.? Of course! We should do these things out of duty and fear and, ultimately, love. Then why has God attached promises of reward with each of the Beatitudes and with so many other admonitions in Scripture? All I can say is because He is gracious and loving and wants to maximize our love for Him and His love for us. *Where your treasure is, there will your heart be also*, Matt. 6:21. If we see Jesus as our treasure, our reward, we will love Him more, and we will experience a greater degree of His love in return.

The bottom line is, we serve a good and gracious God. Was He obligated to implement a system of meritorious reward for faithfulness out of some inherent goodness on our part? Certainly not, but because He has promised to reward, and God cannot lie, He *must* reward — and, in fact, delights to reward — when we lovingly obey and serve him in faithfulness. Is not the Scripture abundantly clear on this point? Are not rewards a valid motivation if kept in proper perspective?

Incidentally, Jesus shared a parable that puts rewards as motivation in proper perspective. In the parable He also dealt with the entitlement mentality.

> For the kingdom of heaven is like unto a man that is an householder, which went out early in the morning to hire labourers into his vineyard. And when he had agreed with the labourers for a penny a day, he sent them into his vineyard. And he went out about the third hour, and saw others standing idle in the marketplace, And said unto them; Go ye also into the vineyard, and whatsoever is right I will give you. And they went their way. Again he went out about the sixth and ninth hour, and did likewise. And about the eleventh hour he went out, and found others standing idle, and saith unto them, Why stand ye here all the day idle? They say unto him, Because no man hath hired us. He saith unto them, Go ye also into the vineyard; and whatsoever is right, that shall ye receive. So when even was come, the lord of the vineyard saith unto his steward, Call the labourers, and give them their hire, beginning from the last unto the first. And when they came that were hired about the eleventh hour, they received every man a penny. But when the first came, they supposed that they should have received more; and they likewise received every man a penny. And when they had received it, they murmured against the goodman of the house, Saying, These last have wrought but one hour, and thou hast made them equal unto us, which have borne the burden and heat of the day. But he answered one of them, and said, Friend, I do thee no wrong: didst not thou agree with me for a penny? Take that thine is, and go thy way: I will give unto this last, even as unto thee. Is it not lawful for me to do what I will with mine own? Is thine eye evil, because I am good? So the last shall be first, and the first last: for many be called, but few chosen. Matt. 20:1-16

I remember when one of our sons was just a little boy. We were having a birthday party and the cake was about to be served. He positioned himself at the front of the line and said, "Me first!" My wife decided to give him some scriptural admonition, quoting Matt. 20:16, *The last shall be first, and the first last*. So he instantly moved to the end of the line and said, "Me last!" — with the expectation, of course, that he would be served first, because the last shall be first. He obviously missed the point! What is the point of this difficult passage?

Humanly speaking, our tendency is to be surprised that both groups of laborers — first hired and last hired — receive the same amount of pay. Why is that? What is Jesus teaching here? I believe the purpose of this parable is to challenge us to think about our motivations for serving Christ. Do we serve with the expectation that all saints will receive the same benefits in eternity? Do we view rewards as a valid motivation?

By way of background to the parable, it is important to understand a common workday in the first century was twelve hours, from 6:00 am to 6:00 pm. A vineyard owner goes into the marketplace before the workday begins — perhaps as early as 5:30 am — to hire workers to harvest his grapes. We find that his first group of workers is hired for an agreed amount of a penny a day, which was the average wage of their day. The workers seem happy with that amount, and they start work at 6:00 am. At the third hour, or 9:00 am, the vineyard owner finds several more workers standing idle in the marketplace and hires them. No specified amount of pay is mentioned. The vineyard owner simply says, *Whatsoever is right I will give you*. These workers also seem content and go to work.

Following the same pattern, the vineyard owner hires several more workers at the sixth hour and the ninth hour, or 12:00 pm and 3:00 pm. Then, finally, at the eleventh hour, or 5:00 pm, he hires still more workers for the last hour of the day. They had been standing idle all day in the marketplace, waiting to be hired. He tells them, *Whatsoever is right, that shall ye receive*.

At 6:00 pm, it is quitting time, and all the men are paid. Curiously, the steward starts by paying the last workers first, that is, the ones hired last. Remarkably, these workers, who had completely trusted the vineyard owner to do right by them, find that he blesses them abundantly, with a full day's wages for only one hour of work. When the laborers who were hired first step up to the cashier for their pay, they expect to receive more, because they see the last group of workers has received a penny. So they expect to receive at least twelve pennies each. But they are shocked when the steward gives them only one penny. In fact, they are upset! They complain that the workers hired at 5:00 pm have only worked one hour, yet their pay is equal to those who have labored in the heat for twelve hours.

As I said earlier, I believe this parable is about rewards and our motivation for serving God. If rewards are a legal payment of sorts for every hour of work done or every act of service performed, then we would have to agree with the disgruntled workers and expect the vineyard owner to pay them more. Otherwise, the Department of Labor Relations might get called in. But that is not how God has set up the system of rewards. It is not a labor contract, paying you for your daily service on His behalf, which is your reasonable service (Rom. 12:1). No, God's rewards are an act of His grace in which He bestows upon you what He sees fit, based on your loving labor for Him.

Here is the key, I believe, to understanding the parable. The focus is not on the amount of pay. The focus is on the attitude of the workers. The workers hired after the first round are all rewarded more graciously, it seems, because of their attitude. They don't have the attitude that their pay rate needs to be legally negotiated with the boss in advance. Nor do they have the attitude that their pay must be equal compensation with everyone else. They don't have the attitude that the boss has a legal requirement to fulfill. That seems to be the attitude of the first group, but not of the other groups hired later.

The men hired at the third hour, the sixth, the ninth, and the eleventh all completely trust the vineyard owner to treat them rightly, as He sees fit. The men hired at the beginning of the day, in contrast, have a legal attitude toward their pay — a "you owe me" attitude. We could refer to them as legalists. Therefore, they (the first) are made last. In what sense are they first? Not merely in the time of their hiring, but also in their attitude – a "you owe me" attitude. They do not labor out of love and trust, like the others. They serve out of a legal, contractual arrangement that demands legal compensation in return.

Incidentally, isn't this akin to those modern Christians who believe that because they are saved — declared legally righteous by God — they are overcomers and, therefore, God has a legal obligation to reward them at the Judgment Seat equally with everyone else? Isn't their expectation very similar to the first group of workers hired in this parable? I wonder if they will have the same murmuring response as these workers, at the Judgment Seat, when they are made to be last, which probably means least in the kingdom (see Matt. 5:19). After saying the first would be last, Jesus added, *For many be called, but few chosen.* To what are they called? They are called to salvation in Christ. To what are they chosen? They are chosen to rule with Christ in the coming kingdom. I wonder if those who are not chosen will be upset with themselves and have to learn to live with regret, when they are given a rebuke and consigned to the darkness outside. If so, it will be because their expectations were wrong and completely unbiblical.

# Chapter 12

---

# The Process of Spiritual Growth

Is it possible to have a sincere heart that wants to please the Lord, accompanied by busyness in ministry and service, and yet perform in the power of the flesh rather than in the Spirit? Absolutely, it is one of the most common deceptions in Christian life and ministry, and Satan loves every minute of it. A lifetime of works-sanctification will undoubtedly result in disinheritance at the Judgment Seat.

When a believer equates works-sanctification with spiritual growth, the result is no growth. At times, that child of God may get in a bind, with no way to turn, and under pressure rely on the Lord for enablement to have victory in time of need. When that happens on occasion, there will be growth. But the growth will not be steady unless this becomes the pattern of life. In other words, spiritual growth will be erratic. On the other hand, when a believer learns to regularly appropriate the enabling power of the Holy Spirit to withstand temptation and endure trials, he will be experiencing regular, steady growth in the Christian life.

Sanctification (i.e., *progressive* sanctification) is the lifelong process of learning to let Christ live His life through us. I used to say it is the process of becoming more like Christ. I don't say that any more, because it is confusing and, therefore, easily misunderstood. Some have abused the meaning of "becoming more like Christ," by mistakenly putting the emphasis on what man must do in the process, rather than focusing on the object, Jesus, and what we must let Him do in us. There is a difference, and it's not as subtle as it seems.

To be sure, sanctification is a process, but we need to yield to God's process, not superimpose our own ideas as to what the process should be. For example, Thomas à Kempis wrote a book in the fifteenth century called, *The Imitation of Christ*, that muddies the waters as to man's involvement in sanctification. So many have fallen prey to the same error. Imitating Christ-like behavior is a biblical concept, if understood and taught correctly (see, for example, 1 Cor. 11:1; Eph. 5:1; 1 Thess. 1:6). However, à Kempis made it a fleshly effort by putting the emphasis on what *we* must *do*, to the exclusion of Christ's enablement. Of ourselves, it is not possible to imitate Christ, no matter how hard we try. Indeed, by "trying" without supernatural enablement, we are injecting fleshly, self-dependence.

Another example is the book *In His Steps*, written by the liberal theologian, Charles Sheldon. Many Christians have no idea that Sheldon did not hold to the fundamentals of the faith but rather promoted a social gospel; he was quite liberal. Yet, how many walk around quoting his statement, "What would Jesus do?" which has been popularized in modern culture by marketing experts who want to prosper from the WWJD cliché, selling bracelets, necklaces, and other paraphernalia. Never mind that Sheldon was totally off base in his theology.

Sheldon's question is dangerous, for it puts man in the driver's seat, rather than the Scriptures, encouraging him to play a sort of spiritual situation ethics. Even a lost man can attempt to play this game. It is really no more than a modern spin on the old, self-dependent "imitation" model of sanctification as proposed by Thomas à Kempis. Both of these books, as noble as they sound, actually promote flesh-dependence.

Again, biblical sanctification is the lifelong process of learning to let Christ live His life through us. It is summed up well in Gal. 2:20. As one submits to the process, he grows spiritually. If one does not understand the process correctly or refuses to yield to the Holy Spirit's working in his life, growth will be stunted. Ongoing, experiential sanctification and spiritual growth are, therefore, closely related concepts.

Spiritual growth is not instantaneous. It happens over time. While I doubt any Christian would dispute that statement (after all, the word *growth* implies a continuing process), some *essentially* argue the opposite: how? By looking to past, life-changing events (a decision during an invitation, a spiritual crisis that precipitated an "I surrender all" moment) as the building blocks of spiritual growth. Others equate participation in religious activities (Bible-reading, prayer, church attendance, soul-winning programs, etc.) with spiritual growth.

While events and religious activities may be catalysts toward change and growth, they certainly don't guarantee growth. Too often, decisions are based on emotion and tend to fade in short time. In the case of religious activities, they can become ritualistic, and tend to salve one's conscience with thoughts such as "this activity makes me spiritual." That is, of course, wrong thinking, and is a deadening form of legalism.

As Americans, we want it now, and we expect it now. The ninety-second turn-around time guaranteed by some fast-food restaurants is classic evidence of our cultural impatience. Unfortunately, we often carry our cultural expectations into our Christianity. We want spiritual maturity now, and we expect it now. Oh, how our eternal God, who is not bound by time, must sigh at our impatience! He is the epitome of patience, and for that we should be truly grateful, because His eternal patience results in His not giving up on us.

Spiritual growth is actually a life-long process that starts when we are saved and continues over time throughout the Christian life. It is gradual and incremental. The Scriptures beautifully define and describe the two key agents of spiritual growth in 2 Pet. 3:18 and the process of spiritual growth in Rom. 5:1-5.

## The Agents of Spiritual Growth

But grow in grace, and in the knowledge of our Lord and Saviour Jesus Christ. 2 Pet. 3:18

## Agent #1: The Engrafted Word

Growth comes, in part, through knowledge of Christ. However, it is not merely knowledge *about* Him. It is *His* knowledge! We already have the mind of Christ, according to 1 Cor. 2:16. How, then, do we appropriate it? By His Spirit whom He has given us. *Now we have received, not the spirit of the world, but the spirit which is of God; that we might know the things that are freely given to us of God,* 1 Cor. 2:12. Of course, the Holy Spirit uses the written Word of God to open up for us the mind of Christ.

I believe the Holy Spirit is the engrafted (implanted) Word, referred to in James 1:21, *Receive with meekness the engrafted word, which is able to save your souls.* How can I conclude the Holy Spirit is the engrafted Word? In Col. 3:16 we are commanded, *Let the word of Christ dwell in you richly.* Many commentators point out the fact that Col. 3:16 is parallel to Eph. 5:18. Indeed, the verses following, in both passages, speak of the same things — spiritual Christians singing, wives submitting, husbands loving, children obeying, employees obeying, etc. — All of which flows from a Spirit-filled life. The parallel to, *Be filled with the Spirit,* Eph. 5:18, is *Let the word of Christ dwell in you richly,* Col. 3:16. In both cases, the reference is to the Holy Spirit — otherwise known as the Word of Christ — dwelling within. He is the engrafted Word, and He is able to save your soul.

The phrase *save your souls,* in its context in James 1:21, does not mean to save from eternal condemnation. It means to sanctify. Thus the child of God is commanded to receive with meekness (i.e, accept with humility) the engrafted Word — the Holy Spirit — who teaches us the written Word and impresses upon our heart truths that we need in order to grow. In other words, He sanctifies us through the Word. Jesus prayed, *Sanctify them through thy truth: thy word is truth,* John 17:17. So the first agent of spiritual growth is the Spirit of God, the engrafted Word, who imparts unto us the mind of Christ through the written Word. *Faith comes by hearing ... the word of God,* Rom. 10:17.

## Agent #2: Grace

Grace is a marvelous spiritual concept. It is a priceless commodity, given to us by God. Ironically, grace is the very thing we most desperately need but most often spurn.

In a salvific sense, grace is God's unmerited favor. But let's get more practical. In a sanctification sense, grace is God's divine enablement to do what He wants us to do. Grace is God giving us what we need to win in every situation — to win over temptation to sin; to win in how we respond to trials; to win in our responses to people; etc.

We need grace every moment of every day. If the righteousness of Christ is our *provision* to win, grace is God's tailor-made *application* of it in every particular situation. He always gives a big dose — *He giveth more grace,* James 4:6. His promise to every Christian: *My grace is sufficient,* 2 Cor. 12:9. The well of grace never runs dry!

If that is not your experience, then you have one of two problems. (Incidentally, the problem is never God; it is always man). The first possible problem is that you may be spurning God's grace by your pride. *God resisteth the proud, but giveth grace to the humble,* James 4:6. Pride comes in many forms, of course, but the kind that typically spurns God's grace is the kind that thinks, "I can do this," or "I will try harder." Any attitude of self-sufficiency or self-dependence will result in spurning God's grace.

The second possible problem is not knowing how to access God's grace, even though the answer is plainly given in the Scriptures. So you must learn the hard way, in the spiritual "school of hard knocks," so to speak. You get into a situation – a trial, a temptation, and you are failing because you have been depending on self. Indeed, you have fallen numerous times in the past, and you are tired of it. Perhaps by being overwhelmed with pressure and sorrow, you finally come to the end of your rope. In desperation, you cry out, "Help me, Lord!" Our gracious God, in His Providence, has allowed you to stumble upon the secret to victory: realizing the utter folly of self-reliance that always fails; turning in complete reliance on Christ who always wins.

The most basic aspect of spiritual growth is learning to depend on the Lord, specifically, the Holy Spirit who lives within. He guides us in all truth, through the Word of God and dispenses grace as needed, to the extent we depend on Him. If only we would learn to continue depending! Is that not the essence of abiding in the vine?

According to 2 Pet. 3:18, the agents of spiritual growth are 1) the engrafted Word, the Holy Spirit, who imparts to us the mind of Christ through the written Word; and 2) grace, which the Holy Spirit dispenses, as needed. How do we access the agent of grace?

> Therefore being justified by faith, we have peace with God through our Lord Jesus Christ: By whom also we have access by faith into this grace wherein we stand, and rejoice in hope of the glory of God. Rom. 5:1-2

## Learning to Access Grace

I have a key that gives entrance to my house. If I lose my key, and no one else is home, I will never get access to the house until I find the key. I can look in the windows. I can imagine everything inside. I can wish I were inside. I can protest my situation and demand that I be given entrance, because I am the rightful owner of the house. But none of these things will gain me entrance. I must have the key.

So it is in the spiritual life with respect to grace. It is freely mine (2 Cor. 12:9; James 4:6). I stand upon it (Rom. 5:2). Nevertheless, I will never experience its application in my life without the key. I can wish for it. I can demand it. I can even cry and bemoan the fact that grace is not at my disposal. But, like my house, I will never get access without the key.

What is the key that unlocks (accesses) grace? It is faith – dependence on God, as opposed to self-dependence. Faith, in this context, is a choice to rely upon God to appropriate His grace in any given situation, whether victory over sin or endurance amidst trials, etc. It is trusting in the Lord with all the heart rather than leaning to our own understanding. It is asking for God's enablement, in any given situation, and then believing He has *already* given it.

When we learn to unlock God's storehouse of grace through the key of dependence on the Holy Spirit, we will be rejoicing in hope (i.e., confident expectation) that God is being glorified in our lives. He is glorified when Christ is living His life through us.

In vs. 3-5 we find the process by which we grow spiritually, or we could say, the means by which we are progressively sanctified.

> And not only so, but we glory in tribulations also: knowing that tribulation worketh patience; And patience, experience; and experience, hope: And hope maketh not ashamed; because the love of God is shed abroad in our hearts by the Holy Ghost which is given unto us. Rom. 5:3-5

## Learning Endurance Through Trials

God teaches us greater dependence on Himself via *tribulations*, or we could say, *trials*. Critical to spiritual growth is learning to respond rightly to trials. God calls it "glorying in tribulations."

The word *tribulations* encompasses a range of troubles: trials, afflictions, suffering, persecution, even daily pressures — traffic pressures, workplace pressures, financial pressures, family pressures, etc. Spiritual growth results when we learn to glory in our troubles. That certainly does not come naturally. Our tendency is to sing the blues rather than sing praise to God amidst troubles. Indeed, the only way a Christian can genuinely rejoice in troubles is by accessing God's grace through dependence on the Holy Spirit. Only then will Jesus live His life through us — and He always responds rightly amidst troubles!

Interestingly, the word *glory* in v. 3 is entirely different than *glory* in v. 2. The Greek word *doxa* is used in v. 2, from which we get the English word *doxology* — an ascription of praise. When you are responding to God in complete dependence amidst trials, you are rejoicing with confident expectation that God is being glorified — praised and honored — by your life.

However, the word *glory* in v. 3 is a different Greek word with an entirely different meaning. It is the idea of boasting in a good sense, or *rejoicing*. In fact, in v. 2 the same Greek word is translated *rejoicing*. Thus, glorying in your tribulations is the idea of rejoicing in your troubles. James 1:4 puts it this way: *Count it all joy when ye fall into diverse temptations* (various trials).

There is no way in the world we can do that of ourselves. Our natural tendency is to chafe at our troubles and to do everything in our power to escape them or sidestep the pain. But a growing Christian will learn (in ever-increasing intensity) to rejoice in his troubles as he depends upon God's grace amidst the troubles.

Is rejoicing in troubles an end in itself? Absolutely not! God tells us why we should rejoice in troubles: *knowing that tribulation worketh patience*. Troubles — to the extent we learn to rejoice in the midst of them — will produce patience in our lives. What good is that? Patience is endurance; it is durative faith, faith that never lets up; faith that keeps trusting; dependence that bears up under the pressure. Our problem, typically, is that we trust God here and there, but we don't trust Him completely and at all times. Troubles help us learn to trust God at all times!

## Learning Confidence Through Experience

A Christian who is regularly depending on God's grace to bear up under the pressure of troubles, is growing. Jesus is living His life through that person. Incidentally, learning patience (endurance) takes time — one trial at a time. That's why in v. 3 God says that patience works (i.e., produces) experience.

Experience is knowledge that is accumulated by participating in something repeatedly, over time. In this case, it's over a lifetime. God doesn't expect us to learn to endure under pressure perfectly in the first few months of the Christian life. It takes years of troubles of varying types for us to learn to trust Him in all things. Thankfully, God is patient with us as we are learning. But we should be learning through trials, not chafing at them, and our learning should be producing an experience and maturity that is invaluable. When we chafe and do not progress, He brings discipline into our lives to help to bring us to the place where we will progress.

Notice in v. 3 where this wonderful experience leads. As you are experiencing God's enabling power to give victory in your troubles, time after time again, you will become a person of hope. Hope is not wishful thinking. As stated earlier, in a biblical sense, hope is confident expectation — not confidence in self, but confidence in God.

Think about it. If you have experienced God giving you grace to respond with joy in trouble after trouble, you are going to become a person who *confidently expects* God to work all the time — not only in your life, but also in the lives of others. You will be consistently joyful; you will be consistently optimistic. The optimism is not merely a positive mental attitude. It is a confident spirit, based on God, whom you know to be true *all the time!*

People who live in the realm of hope are not ashamed. In fact, hope is so confident in the Lord that it is bold; it does not cower in fear. This is not merely personality boldness; it is boldness that only the Holy Spirit can produce. It is the kind of boldness that endures under the most intense form of troubles — persecution, even death for Christ. The Christian who has learned through experience to rejoice amidst troubles by depending on God's grace will be ready to meet the persecution with boldness.

## Learning to Love as Jesus Loves

The climax of the passage — the ultimate end of spiritual growth — is found in v. 5, *The love of God is shed abroad in our hearts by the Holy Spirit.* God wants us all to mature to the point of becoming genuinely loving Christians, but agape-type love is rarely found in the lives of most Christians. It is seen in those who are described as being like Jesus, because Jesus is living His life through them.

Love (as a way of life, not merely a burst here or there) is characteristic in the lives of those Christians who have learned to depend upon God's grace to enable them to rejoice in their troubles, over a period of time, so that it becomes their experience. Because they have so experienced God's deliverance for victory over and over again, they are confident people in the Lord, expecting God to do great things all the time. After living in that realm of life for some period of time, hope graduates to love, the ultimate.

Three of the key words in this passage are *faith* (v. 2), *hope* (v. 4), and *love* (v. 5) — the very three words the apostle Paul uses to sum up the Christian life at the end of 1 Cor. 13. These are the three things that matter, no doubt the three things that will survive God's fire at the Judgment Seat. Everything else that is accomplished in life apart from faith or hope or love will be burned up!

The most basic element of this triplet is *faith* — dependence on God — the very thing that unlocks God's grace. Ironically, it is the starting point of a sanctified life, yet so few Christians seem to grasp the concept of depending on the Lord for a rejoicing spirit amidst their troubles.

No wonder Christians do not bear up under pressure. No wonder Christians are lacking in confident expectation, the divine optimism that results in boldness that is eager to suffer and die for Jesus. No wonder Christianity is bereft of self-sacrificing, unconditional love. The problem is that so many, despite being saved for decades, have never really progressed in sanctification because they have never learned to appropriate God's grace by faith. Oh, may we see our great need and learn to grow in grace! The words *well done* are at stake.

# Chapter 13

# Not Hurt of the Second Death

I used to think all Christians are overcomers by nature of their position in Christ as children of God. But I have since learned the Bible teaches otherwise. Only faithful servants are overcomers. What is an overcomer? An overcomer is one who is victorious. In fact, the Greek word is *nike* – which also happened to be the name of the Greek goddess of victory. In Roman mythology, she was called Victoria.

In the spiritual life, we are in a battle. As we pointed out in Chapter 1, we wrestle not against flesh and blood, but against principalities and powers (a spiritual realm). Yet we should not become anxious, for we have been given all the necessary provision for winning the battle. The provision resides in our spirit. He is called Holy Spirit.

If we appropriate our provision for conquering the battles of the soul, we will be victorious. If we choose not to appropriate our provision, we will not be victorious in our soul. Over the course of a lifetime, believers establish a pattern of either victory or defeat — or we could call it walking in the flesh or walking in the Spirit. Those who have a constant pattern of defeat will not be declared overcomers at the Judgment Seat and will receive a negative reward. Whereas, those who have learned victory over the world, the flesh, and the devil will be declared victors and rewarded abundantly at the Bema. Of course, there are degrees of rewards too.

In my opinion, an error has crept into the church in modern times, and it is the error that all Christians are overcomers by way of their standing in Christ. Follow that line of thinking out to its logical conclusion. If all Christians are overcomers, then there is no battle, for the soul has already reached its goal of complete sanctification, and no Christian could ever do anything to displease the Lord. If all Christians are overcomers, then why was Paul concerned about becoming a castaway? Why did he press toward the mark? Why are we warned not to lose our reward (2 John 8)? Why are we cautioned about being ashamed when meeting Jesus (1 John 2:28)? If all Christians are overcomers, then what is the purpose of the crowns and the rewards in Rev. 2-3? What is the purpose of the admonitions regarding the Judgment Seat and the prospect of suffering loss?

The error of assuming all Christians are overcomers has fueled a lackadaisical attitude toward Christian living. It has unwittingly promoted licentious behavior, on the basis that we are all victors. What a huge mistake! So in the twenty-first century we are faced with multitudes of Christians who do not take the Judgment Seat seriously and who live unto themselves. The intent of this book is to wake up Christians to the truth and to help them prepare to hear *well done* at the Judgment Seat by becoming overcomers now.

The passage that is typically used to try to prove that all Christians are overcomers is 1 John 5:1-5:

> 1 Whosoever believeth that Jesus is the Christ is born of God: and every one that loveth him that begat loveth him also that is begotten of him.
> 2 By this we know that we love the children of God, when we love God, and keep his commandments.
> 3 For this is the love of God, that we keep his commandments: and his commandments are not grievous.
> 4 For whatsoever is born of God overcometh the world: and this is the victory that overcometh the world, even our faith.
> 5 Who is he that overcometh the world, but he that believeth that Jesus is the Son of God.

Typical of John in the epistles, he states a positional truth as motivation for living out the practical application. In other words, John points to the provision within our spirit as the means of finding victory in our soul. He references the positional truth, the provision in our spirit, in v. 1a — *Whoever believes that Jesus is the Christ is born of God* — and in v. 4a — *Whoever is born of God overcomes the world*. That is positional truth, but it's not automatic; it does not necessarily equate to the experience of one's life and behavior. Granted, believers are the only ones to have the prospect of becoming over-comers (v. 5), but experiential overcoming is not guaranteed; it's conditional, based on obedience and faithful service. Yet we have no ability to obey of ourselves, so we must access our provision so that we can obey (i.e., *keep His commandments*, v. 3). How do we access our provision to obey? Look at the end of v. 4 — by faith. As we noted in Chapter 12, the apostle Paul says the same in Rom. 5:2 — we access God's grace by faith. Peter says the same in 2 Pet. 1 — we have been given everything we need to be partakers with Christ in His divine nature and escape the world's corruptions. How do we access it? *Whereby are given unto us exceeding great and precious promises*, 2 Pet. 1:4 — and then Peter instructs us to add to our faith. The context of the passage dictates that it is sanctifying faith, not saving faith.

Faith is the victory that overcomes the world. But, again, it's not automatic in terms of daily experience. You must depend upon the Spirit of God who lives within your spirit in order to be victorious in your soul. Thus, John is giving us provisional truth as the basis for our practical behavior, and he's essentially urging us to access what we have by faith in order to be victorious over the world, the flesh, and the devil. He is not saying that all Christians are overcomers in the realm of their soul, their behavior. What he's saying is that all Christians have the ability to become overcomers, because of Christ who lives within the spirit aspect of their being.

## Rewards Promised to Overcomers

We now need to go to Rev. 2-3 to see the special rewards that are promised to overcomers. These are the letters Jesus gives to the seven churches. They were seven actual churches during John's day, spread throughout Asia Minor, which is modern Turkey. They represent believers throughout church history. Jesus tells each one of these churches what He thinks of their spiritual condition. Then He promises a reward to those who take heed to the admonitions He gives to the churches. Those who are rewarded are called overcomers. The text makes it obvious that these rewards are conditional, based on behavior. So this has nothing to do with initial salvation from condemnation. It has everything to do with soul-salvation, or what we commonly call progressive sanctification. These rewards clearly are not for all saints. They are only for those who overcome experientially.

Let me forewarn you that some of these rewards are enigmas, but Jesus has put them in His word for us to ponder, nonetheless. Incidentally, I don't believe our Lord wants us to ignore these passages, simply because they are puzzling. Surely that would displease Him. We must work through them and arrive at some conclusions, even if we can't be dogmatic. In this chapter and the next, I will share my conclusions, but I freely admit there continues to be an aura of mystique about them in my mind.

Our purpose is not to exposit each of the seven letters in detail. However, we are going to explore each of the seven rewards given in these letters. In this chapter we will cover the first two, and then examine the other five rewards in the next chapter.

### Reward #1: Overcomers will eat of the tree of life.

> To him that overcometh will I give to eat of the tree of life, which is in the midst of the paradise of God. Rev. 2:7

Knowing that all believers possess eternal life, what is the benefit of being able to eat of the tree of life? Remember that the tree of life was in the Garden of Eden, but it has disappeared for the past six thousand years and will return in the age to come. But it will not be on Earth; it will be in the midst of the paradise of God. In other words, it will be in the heavenly Jerusalem, the city of reward, which is only for the faithful, so that only the faithful ones will be able to eat of it.

What is the purpose of the tree of life?

In the midst of the street of it, and on either side of the river, was there the tree of life, which bare twelve manner of fruits, and yielded her fruit every month: and the leaves of the tree were for the healing of the nations. Rev. 22:2

This seems to be describing a massive tree that bears twelve different fruits throughout the year. It does not grow on Earth; it grows in the middle of God's paradise (Rev. 2:7), which seems to be a reference to the city of reward. Since only the faithful will be in that realm, they will be the only ones allowed to eat of the tree.

Apparently, the tree of life has a twofold purpose: various fruits that brings a quality of life for those who partake, and leaves that provide healing for the nations. Perhaps this could imply physical healing for those in the earthly realm of the kingdom, which only the faithful, who reside in the heavenly city, will be able to administer to those on Earth. The millennial kingdom will be characterized by healing and great power worked by the faithful ones. What a magnificent tree!

The Old Testament speaks of the tree of life symbolically.

She (wisdom) is a tree of life to them that lay hold upon her: and happy is every one that retaineth her. Prov. 3:18

Wisdom is likened unto a tree of life, a quality of life far beyond average. In the age to come, the tree of life may impart wisdom and knowledge to the faithful ones who are with Christ in the heavenly Jerusalem, so they will be more equipped to administer affairs on Earth and know more of the ways of God. Perhaps this wisdom will also give the faithful ones a greater opportunity to know Christ intimately.

The fruit of the righteous is a tree of life; and he that winneth souls is wise. Prov. 11:30

I believe "soul-winning," in this context, is not merely pointing lost people to the Savior but is predominantly the idea of discipling saved people so that their soul becomes saved (i.e., sanctified) at the Judgment Seat. Those who do that are wise. The fruit of their life and ministry is a tree of life, and presumably, they will eat of the tree of life in the age to come. A passage in Daniel, while not specifically mentioning the tree of life, promises similar reward:

> And they that be wise shall shine as the brightness of the firmament; and they that turn many to righteousness as the stars for ever and ever. Dan. 12:3

Those who teach others about the kingdom and help those saints to get their soul ready for the Judgment Seat will receive great reward. They will shine brightly and will eat of the tree of life in the heavenly Jerusalem. What a glorious reward!

### Reward #2: Overcomers will be given a crown of life and will not be hurt of the second death.

> Behold, the devil shall cast some of you into prison, that ye may be tried; and ye shall have tribulation ten days: be thou faithful unto death, and I will give thee a crown of life ... He that overcometh shall not be hurt of the second death. Rev. 2:10-11

This is a rather peculiar reward. For it implies that those who are not deemed faithful will not receive a crown of life and will be hurt by the second death. But how can that be? We know the second death for the unsaved is the lake of fire. Saved people are eternally secure, of course, and will not spend eternity in the lake of fire. How do we make sense of this? The tendency of many dispensational preachers and teachers has been to see this statement and say, "That can't be!" and then assume that all Christians are overcomers, making this promise apply to all saints. Frankly, that is a hasty assumption and ignores the teaching of the Scriptures. When we come to a difficult passage like this, we must not invent a nice-sounding theological system so that we can fit certain verses into our paradigm. Rather, we must wrestle with the verse and see what God is saying, even if it goes against the grain of what we have been taught!

What is meant by *second death* in this context? It's obviously not eternity in a lake of fire. The lost spend eternity in the lake of fire because their spirit never becomes saved from eternal condemnation. But our spirit has been saved, so we do not face eternal condemnation. However, there is the very real prospect of our soul not being saved (sanctified), and if that is the case at the Judgment Seat, we will receive a negative reward. Part of that reward is apparently being hurt of the second death. But what does that mean?

## Baptism in Fire

Let's begin to unravel this by reading the words of John the Baptist.

> I indeed baptize you with water unto repentance: but he that cometh after me is mightier than I, whose shoes I am not worthy to bear: he shall baptize you with the Holy Ghost, and with fire. Matt. 3:11

More specifically, Greek lexical aids suggest that the last phrase of this verse could also be translated, "He shall baptize you *in* the Holy Spirit and *in* fire." The English word *baptize* is actually a transliteration (not a translation) of the Greek word *baptizo*, which means to immerse or submerge. It was the word used of ships that sank at sea. Thus, when John baptized, he immersed. He didn't merely baptize *with* water; he baptized *in* water. John announced that Jesus would immerse in Holy Spirit and in fire. Baptism in the Holy Spirit occurs at salvation of the spirit (1 Cor. 12:13). When does baptism in fire occur? Presumably, at the Judgment Seat, when Jesus determines whether or not the believer's soul has been saved (i.e., sanctified unto completion).

> Every man's work shall be made manifest: for the day shall declare it, because it shall be revealed by fire; and the fire shall try every man's work of what sort it is. If any man's work abide which he hath built thereupon, he shall receive a reward. If any man's work shall be burned, he shall suffer loss: but he himself shall be saved; yet so as by fire. 1 Cor. 3:13-15

> But that which beareth thorns and briers is rejected, and is nigh unto cursing; whose end is to be burned. Heb. 6:8

> If a man abide not in me, he is cast forth as a branch, and is withered; and men gather them, and cast them into the fire, and they are burned. John 15:6

Apparently, Jesus will baptize (immerse) in fire at the Judgment Seat. Some will be burned; that is, their works will be consumed. In that sense, they will be hurt by the fire. Could this be a reference to His fiery eyes (Rev. 19:12)? Perhaps, but it is not likely, because the believer will apparently be baptized (immersed) in the fire, and eyes of fire don't seem to carry the idea of immersion in fire. My opinion is that it must be referring to a furnace or pool of fire.

So let's consider a *possible* scenario. We meet Jesus at the Judgment Seat. We all must pass through (be immersed in) the fire. What fire? We don't know for sure, because the Bible does not give the specifics. Could it be the lake of fire, also known as the furnace of fire? I cannot prove that, but are you able to disprove it? Is it that far-fetched? Consider Shadrach, Meshach, and Abednego. Their lives so pleased the Lord that He preserved them in Nebuchadnezzar's fiery furnace. In essence, God declared, *Well done!* Despite their baptism in fire, they were not harmed, not even singed. In fact, they emerged from the furnace not even smelling of smoke. For their faithfulness, God rewarded them with positions of rulership in Nebuchadnezzar's kingdom.

How could a Christian possibly be hurt by the second death? From the verses above, we know conclusively that every Christian will pass through a fire of sorts. Could that fire be the lake of fire, the second death? At that point in time, the lake of fire will not yet be populated by the unsaved; that happens after the millennium. The saved will not remain in the lake of fire, of course, but will merely pass through — be immersed in — the second death, according to the model I am proposing. After passing through the furnace of fire, some will come out unscathed (like the three Hebrew men in Babylon), for their works will be of the quality of gold, silver, and precious stones. The fire will not hurt them. It will be as if they are wearing asbestos suits. But other Christians will lose everything. That is, the quality of their work being of wood, hay, stubble — consumables — it will be devoured in the fire. They will be hurt of the second death, stripped of any prospect of reward. They will be saved, yet so as by (through) fire.

How do we explain their salvation? Because their spirit has been saved, made righteous, it must survive the fire or the second death. But since their soul was never saved, it will be consumed in the fire. Jesus said, "Whoever saves his life (soul) now will lose it then." As we said in an earlier chapter, to lose one's soul is to lose one's reward. In other words, there will be negative recompense at the Bema.

While I cannot be dogmatic about the scenario proposed above, it is a possible solution to the question, "How can saints be hurt of the second death?"

## Spiritual Death For the Saint

We can easily connect spiritual death now (for the saint) with death of the soul, so to speak, at the Bema.

> For to be carnally minded is death; but to be spiritually minded is life and peace. Because the carnal mind is enmity against God: for it is not subject to the law of God, neither indeed can be. So then they that are in the flesh cannot please God. Rom. 8:6-8

These verses are written to born again believers, warning that carnality (continued fleshly behavior) results in spiritual death here and now, but spiritual-mindedness results in abundant life and peace. The bottom line is those who live in carnality do not please God in the present. Needless to say, the present impacts the future.

> For if ye live after the flesh, ye shall die: but if ye through the Spirit do mortify the deeds of the body, ye shall live. Rom. 8:13

If you live according to the flesh (in the present), you will die (in the future); you will be hurt of the second death. But if you appropriate the provision of the Holy Spirit in your spirit, and thereby put to death the works of the flesh (in the present — Gal. 5:19-20), you will live (in the future). In the context of Rom. 8, the future death or future life are not relative to the spirit, for Paul is speaking to saved people. Paul is referring to matters of the soul which impact sanctification and reward. Thus, death or life relate to quality of living in the coming kingdom. Death for the saint equates to loss of reward and a portion in the darkness outside of His bright ruling realm. Life (i.e., the crown of life and eating of the tree of life) is the reward of faithful saints, an inheritance in His city of reward as the bride of the Lamb, ruling together with Him for eternity. Consider the following table that distinguishes between two types of saints.

| Carnal | Spiritual |
|---|---|
| Friend of the world | Friend of God |
| Ashamed of Christ | Bold & unashamed |
| Lives by sight | Lives by faith |
| Disobedient and slothful | Obedient and faithful |
| Patterns of defeat — overcome | Patterns of victory — overcomer |
| Spiritual death | Spiritual life |
| Soul lost at the Bema | Soul saved at the Bema |
| Hurt of the second death | Inherit a crown of life |
| Outer darkness | City of reward |
| Mundane existence on Earth | Rule and reign in the heavenliness |
| No rewards | Rewards promised for overcomers |
| "Thou wicked & slothful servant" | "Well done, good & faithful servant" |

You don't have to be hurt by the second death. The choice is yours. You can appropriate your provision, given to all saints, and live the Christ life. Jesus offers to fill you through His Holy Spirit and enable you to obey Him, and He offers you a reward. So why not choose life?

# Chapter 14

---

# Rewards for Overcomers

In Chapter 13 we studied the first two rewards promised to overcomers in Rev. 2-3.

**Reward #1: Overcomers will eat of the tree of life.** What must you overcome to receive this reward? The church at Ephesus had left their first love (Rev. 2:4). They were doctrinally solid and busy about the work of the ministry, but they had no life, no spark. They were characterized by dead orthodoxy. If you want to inherit the first reward, you must not leave your first love, or if you have left it, return to it and never leave it again.

**Reward #2: A crown of life and not hurt by the second death.** What must you overcome to receive this reward? The reward of the crown of life is preceded by an admonition to *be ... faithful unto death*, Rev. 2:10. The church at Smyrna was under great persecution. The temptation was to lose heart and give up. God wants you to endure faithfully unto death despite any sufferings or persecutions. Don't lose heart! A crown of life awaits.

In this chapter we will discover five more rewards. Some of them are multi-faceted. It is important to remember these rewards are given in the letters to the seven churches in Rev. 2-3. These churches represent born again believers throughout the entire church age. In other words, the letters are like a mirror. As we read them we should ask God to show us how we appear spiritually to Him, and we should hear what the Spirit is saying to the churches. We should take heed, so that we can be rewarded. Indeed, He wants us to be rewarded, for He is glorified when we are rewarded.

**Reward #3: Overcomers will eat of the hidden manna and will receive a new name on a white stone.**

> To him that overcometh will I give to eat of the hidden manna, and will give him a white stone, and in the stone a new name written, which no man knoweth saving he that receiveth it. Rev. 2:17

Manna, of course, was the nourishing food God gave to the children of Israel while they were in the wilderness. It was nutritious and healthy and kept them from malnourishment. It was loaded with all the necessary vitamins and minerals. Nowadays, in a spiritual sense, children of God can receive spiritual manna from the Word of God if they will choose to dine and feast regularly on the Holy Scriptures. So many choose not to do so and become malnourished.

We must remember that in the age to come we will also have bodies and will have, as a very minimum, the ability to eat, as Jesus did in His resurrected body. We may even have some need to eat; we don't know. The point is that overcomers will receive a healthy food that will have both physical and spiritual properties — genetically produced by God to have the greatest effect. It is called *hidden* manna — not that the food itself is hidden, but the physical health and spiritual truth and wisdom it imparts are hidden from others, I believe. Perhaps this heavenly food will enable us to know incredible truths that are not recorded in the Word of God. Maybe it will fortify us for ministering to those on Earth who were deemed unfaithful at the Judgment Seat. We don't know much about it, but we do know it has something to do with sustenance in the age to come — probably physical and spiritual. It sounds very exciting and intriguing.

Overcomers are also promised a white stone, containing a new name. This is rather peculiar. We think of Joseph, to whom the Pharaoh gave a ring and robes and a gold chain and a royal chariot and a new name and made him prime minister. Daniel was made *a great man* by Nebuchadnezzar and given *many great gifts* and *made ruler over the whole province of Babylon and ... over all the wise men.* He was also given a new name (Dan. 4:8). These men were overcomers, and they represent overcomers at the Judgment Seat. Jesus will give a very special gift to overcomers, not a mere trinket, but a precious white stone, undoubtedly of great value in God's eyes. The color represents purity and holiness.

On Earth we have things such as employee identification badges and key fobs which, when scanned, give access to certain places where others are not allowed to go. Perhaps the white stone is a heavenly version of that — an access device, of sorts — giving access to the city of reward and other special places in Heaven and Earth. Maybe it will give access to secret spiritual truths. What is absolutely thrilling is that it will be personalized to the faithful one, for his or her new name will be inscribed on it. The new name will be given by God and perhaps will sum up God's thoughts about that one's character. It will be a secret, not publicly known, but manifested only to that individual, implying a special closeness with Jesus.

What must you overcome to receive this reward? You must hate worldliness and not be a man worshiper (Rev. 2:14-15). That was the problem of the church at Pergamos. They had in their congregation some who held to the doctrine of Balaam, a reference to the Old Testament apostate prophet who taught the Israelites to love and intermingle with the world. They had others that held to the doctrine of the Nicolaitans, and one key aspect of their doctrine was elevating certain personalities. Doesn't that sound like the modern church of Jesus Christ?

### Reward #4: Overcomers will rule over the nations and be given the morning star.

> He that overcometh, and keepeth my works unto the end, to him will I give power over the nations: And he shall rule them with a rod of iron; as the vessels of a potter shall they be broken to shivers: even as I received of my Father. And I will give him the morning star. Rev. 2:26-28

This is the very purpose for which we were created. As we learned in Chapter 1, when God created Adam, He instructed the first man to have dominion over the earth. Adam forfeited that right to Satan when he sinned, and Satan became the prince of this world. Christ defeated Satan at the cross, but Jesus does not presently rule this earth. He will do so when He comes again and establishes His millennial kingdom. But only His faithful ones will rule with Him, those who suffer with Him (Rom. 8:17; 2 Tim. 2:12). It is audacious to think Christ would allow unfaithful saints, an impure bride, to rule with Him.

The other part of the promise is that overcomers will be given the morning star. The morning star is Jesus; there is no doubt about that.

> I Jesus have sent mine angel to testify unto you these things in the churches. I am the root and the offspring of David, and the bright and morning star. Rev. 22:16

In what sense will overcomers be given the morning star? We don't know for sure; it's a bit of a mystery. In the context of ruling, it may mean the overcomer is given the authority of Jesus to rule as if Jesus Himself were ruling. Some commentators suggest that Jesus as morning star is a reference to His rapturing the church in advance of the resurrections to follow. If that is the case, then perhaps this could be a promise that in the rapture Jesus will be much closer and personal to the faithful ones. Then it would be a reference to the out-resurrection, the up-calling to the city of reward for ruling that will be discussed in the next chapter. The bottom line is that we don't know, but it will be exciting!

What must you overcome to receive this reward? The church at Thyatira had fornicated religiously and spiritually. It could be they were becoming ecumenical, cooperating in ministry with unbelievers. God promises a reward if you will remain separated and *hold fast* to truth until Jesus returns (Rev. 2:25). Furthermore, you must keep Christ's works to the end, that is, continue faithful in obedience and service throughout your life, depending all the while on Christ who lives within. This reward is for those who allow Christ to accomplish His works through them.

**Reward #5: Overcomers will be clothed in white, their names will not be blotted out of the book of life, and Jesus will confess them before the Father.**

> He that overcometh, the same shall be clothed in white raiment; and I will not blot out his name out of the book of life, but I will confess his name before my Father, and before his angels. Rev. 3:5

Why will the overcomers be clothed in white? Incidentally, there is a tendency to assume that all Christians will be wearing white robes, but as we discussed in Chapter 9, Rev. 19:8 clarifies that *the fine, white linen is the righteousnesses* (plural) *of the saints.* In other words, the qualification for receiving white robes of righteousness is not merely the imputed righteousness that all saints possess in Christ. The imparted righteousness that comes through progressive sanctification is also required. The robes, quite literally, are a representation of each saint's behavioral righteousness. If you have been carnal and not faithful to the Lord in obedience, you will not receive white robes of righteousness. The white robes will apparently only be worn by overcomers, as we find in the above promise.

I believe these robes are connected with glory. The whiteness is the idea of brightness in varying degrees, a reflection of Christ's brightness. Remember how Jesus on the Mount of Transfiguration glowed with an intense whiteness/ brightness? (See Matt. 17:2). That was His glorified body that will be displayed in the heavenly Jerusalem. He shares His brightness with His faithful ones in varying degrees, depending on their intensity of faithfulness. The apostle Paul spoke about this.

> There is one glory of the sun, and another glory of the moon, and another glory of the stars: for one star differeth from another star in glory. So also is the resurrection of the dead. 1 Cor. 15:41-42

What a magnificent concept – white robes for overcomers that glow with the brightness of Christ! This particular reward also includes not being blotted out of the book of life, but rather having Jesus confess your name before the Father. Again, this is not a promise for all Christians but for overcomers. But this poses a bit of a conundrum. Aren't the names of all Christians in the book of life? And aren't we all eternally secure? The answer is "yes" to both questions. How, then, can the name of a believer become blotted out of the book of life?

The Scriptures seem to use the book of life in at least three different ways, so perhaps there are three different books. Or perhaps there is one book of life with different chapters or sections. Or perhaps (using the illustration of a ledger or spreadsheet), there is one book of life containing rows and columns, with the names of people on rows and checkmarks in the appropriate columns for all the characteristics that apply. That may sound confusing or even outlandish to some, but perhaps it will become clearer if we piece together several passages of Scripture.

### Book #1: Physical life (Body)

> Thine eyes did see my substance, yet being unperfect; and in thy book all my members were written, which in continuance were fashioned, when as yet there was none of them. Ps. 139:16

The psalmist David recognized that he had been written in God's "book" at the point of conception. Thus, one of God's books records physical life.

> Yet now, if thou wilt forgive their sin—; and if not, blot me, I pray thee, out of thy book which thou hast written. And the Lord said unto Moses, Whosoever hath sinned against me, him will I blot out of my book. Exod. 32:32-33

When the children of Israel sinned so grievously in making the golden calf, God was about to destroy them, but Moses interceded and asked God to spare them, blotting his name instead out of God's book, presumably the book of life. Some scholars believe Moses was requesting that he experience an untimely death in place of the Israelites. He certainly wasn't asking to go to Hell. That would not glorify God. He was asking to die, so his countrymen might live. It seems this first book of life is focused on the body — recording life and blotting it out at death.

## Book #2: Eternal life (Spirit)

> Notwithstanding in this rejoice not, that the spirits are subject unto you; but rather rejoice, because your names are written in heaven. Luke 10:20

> For our conversation is in heaven; from whence also we look for the Saviour, the Lord Jesus Christ: Phil. 3:20

> And I intreat thee also, true yokefellow, help those women which laboured with me in the gospel … whose names are in the book of life. Phil. 4:3

These verses deal with the saved having their names written in the book of life, referring to the salvation of the spirit, the gift of eternal life. But what about the lost?

> And all that dwell upon the earth shall worship him (antichrist), whose names are not written in the book of life of the Lamb slain from the foundation of the world. Rev. 13:8

> And whosoever was not found written in the book of life was cast into the lake of fire. Rev. 20:15

The lost are not written in this book of life, for it deals with spiritual life, everlasting life.

## Book #3: Spiritual life (Soul)

> He that overcometh, the same shall be clothed in white raiment; and I will not blot out his name out of the book of life, but I will confess his name before my Father, and before his angels. Rev. 3:5

> And there shall in no wise enter into it any thing that defileth, neither whatsoever worketh abomination, or maketh a lie: but they which are written in the Lamb's book of life. Rev. 21:27

> And if any man shall take away from the words of the book of this prophecy, God shall take away his part out of the book of life, and out of the holy city, and from the things which are written in this book. Rev. 22:19

The above verses demonstrate the possibility of a third book, which seems to be based on the soul and matters of sanctification. Those written in the book will be rewarded.

Those not written in the book or blotted out of the book will not be rewarded. Jesus will not confess them before His Father in Heaven. Eternal life is not at stake, but all prospect of reward is forfeited.

Perhaps instead of three books, God has one book with rows and columns, much like a ledger or spreadsheet.

## A Possible Scenario

Suppose when a person is conceived his name is added to the book of life and a check mark is placed next to his name in the column that is labeled *body*. When he is born again another check mark is added to the book of life in the columns labeled *spirit* and *soul*. But let's say that over the course of the man's life, he lives for self — carnal and fleshly in behavior, not as a faithful servant — so that his soul does not become sanctified by the end of his life. Jesus blots out the check mark from the book of life that had specified spiritual life in the soul. The man is disinherited from ruling in the kingdom and given a negative verdict at the Judgment Seat. I believe that is what Rev. 3:5 is implying will happen to those who do not overcome. Non-overcomers do not lose salvation, for that is impossible. But their names are blotted off the list of those qualified to receive inheritance.

For those who remain as firstborn sons, inheritors of the kingdom, Jesus will confess them before the Father and before the angels. Why the angels? Because the faithful will rule over angels (1 Cor. 6:3). What must you overcome to receive this reward? Several things are indicated in the text of Rev. 3:

- Spiritual deadness – v. 1
- Imperfect works – v. 2
- Unpreparedness to meet Christ – v. 3
- Soiled garments – v. 4

At the time of Christ's meeting with John the apostle, only a few in the church of Sardis were worthy of reward. Would that be said of the twenty-first century church of Jesus Christ?

## Reward #6: Overcomers are made pillars in God's temple and Christ's name is written on them.

> Him that overcometh will I make a pillar in the temple of my God, and he shall go no more out: and I will write upon him the name of my God, and the name of the city of my God, which is new Jerusalem, which cometh down out of heaven from my God: and I will write upon him my new name. Rev. 3:12

The word *pillar* means tower and conveys the idea of strength and stability. Overcomers will become spiritual towers in the heavenly temple. The psalmist said, *I had rather be a doorkeeper in the house of my God, than to dwell in the tents of wickedness,* Ps. 84:10. He was conveying his desire to be in the very lowliest position in the temple, as long as he could be dwelling with God and not in the tabernacles of the wicked. But God lovingly promises something much better to His faithful ones — not merely a place as doorkeepers, but pillars. What an honor!

Furthermore, in contradistinction to the followers of antichrist during the tribulation, who will take the mark of the beast, these faithful ones will take the name of Jesus upon them and will be marked as the holy priests in the Old Testament. They will be given a special place in the city of reward, the heavenly city, reserved only for the faithful. I would encourage you to read Rev. 21-22 to get a complete description of this heavenly place of ruling, for it is magnificent.

What must you overcome to receive this reward? You must keep the Word of God (v. 8). Stand upon it, embrace it, live it, and teach it. Never deny Christ, even when persecuted. Confess Him before men. Stay faithful in perseverance unto the end. Jesus had mostly good things to say to the church of Philadelphia, and He admonished them to let no man take their crown (v. 11), implying that if they stayed on course, they would inherit rulership. May we all be faithful!

## Reward #7: Overcomers will sit with Christ in His throne.

> To him that overcometh will I grant to sit with me in my throne, even as I also overcame, and am set down with my Father in his throne. Rev. 3:21

Following His resurrection and ascension Jesus was exalted to the right hand of the Father, a place of authority and power.

> That ye may know ... what is the exceeding greatness of his power to us-ward who believe, according to the working of his mighty power, Which he wrought in Christ, when he raised him from the dead, and set him at his own right hand in the heavenly places, Far above all principality, and power, and might, and dominion, and every name that is named, not only in this world, but also in that which is to come: And hath put all things under his feet, and gave him to be the head over all things to the church. Eph. 1:18-22

One of the present positional benefits we all enjoy as believers is that we are seated with Christ in a spiritual sense on His throne in the heavenlies.

> And hath raised us up together, and made us sit together in heavenly places in Christ Jesus: Eph. 2:6

Think of it! We are presently seated with Christ in the heavenlies, a place of great power and authority. Jesus wants us to claim our position of authority in Him over the enemy, by faith, in this present world. So few believers even realize they possess such delegated authority, much less claim it. Yet there is much at stake. Those who regularly appropriate the spiritual power of Christ's throne in this present world will be deemed overcomers and will be given the special privilege of sitting with him in a ruling sense in the world to come. What a high and holy privilege! I can think of no greater honor than sitting with Jesus on His throne, as His co-regent.

Notice in Rev. 3:21 Jesus says, *even as I overcame*. Jesus was an overcomer. He wants to be the firstborn among many brethren (Rom. 8:29). Revel in this truth. This is when the angelic host of Satan will be deposed and Jesus will take rule over Heaven and Earth, along with His faithful servants. Do you want to sit with Him on His throne? If so, are you willing to pay the price?

What must you overcome to receive this reward? The church of Laodicea was a lukewarm, complacent church. They cared more for the things they could see than the things they could not see (the eternal realm). They were materialistic.

Satan tries to lure us through our western culture to love the world, just like the Laodiceans. If you want to be an overcomer, you must not live as a lukewarm Christian (Rev. 3:15). Stop depending on things, the material things of this world, and start depending on Christ (v. 18). Open the door of your soul to Christ and let Him take control (v. 20). Oh the fellowship you can have with Jesus if you will let Him in. You will enjoy His presence now and in the world to come.

# Chapter 15

# Otherworldly Ambitions

The book of Philippians is one of Paul's prison epistles, written from Rome near the end of his life. In this marvelous letter we find the heart cry of Paul with respect to rewards. He beautifully expresses his desire to know Christ intimately and to please Him. The essence of the passage is Paul's longing to hear the words, *Well done,* at the Judgment Seat and to be worthy of ruling with Christ in His kingdom. The apostle expresses his heart with the saints at Philippi, with the intent that they have the same burning desire. As we read the passage below, may we all yearn for our Lord's approval. May we have the attitude, "Lord, do this work in me too! I want to go all the way with you in discipleship!"

7 But what things were gain to me, those I counted loss for Christ.
8 Yea doubtless, and I count all things but loss for the excellency of the knowledge of Christ Jesus my Lord: for whom I have suffered the loss of all things, and do count them but dung, that I may win Christ,
9 And be found in him, not having mine own righteousness, which is of the law, but that which is through the faith of Christ, the righteousness which is of God by faith:
10 That I may know him, and the power of his resurrection, and the fellowship of his sufferings, being made conformable unto his death;
11 If by any means I might attain unto the resurrection of the dead.

12 Not as though I had already attained, either were already perfect: but I follow after, if that I may apprehend that for which also I am apprehended of Christ Jesus.
13 Brethren, I count not myself to have apprehended: but this one thing I do, forgetting those things which are behind, and reaching forth unto those things which are before,
14 I press toward the mark for the prize of the high calling of God in Christ Jesus.
Phil. 3:7-14

In order to rightly understand this passage, we must consider the context. Paul is writing to believers. How do we know that? Paul starts chapter three with the words, *Finally, my brethren*. Children of God refer to their spiritual siblings as "brethren." These are saved people, predominantly Gentiles. I am not going to take the time to exposit the entire chapter, so let me get to the heart of the matter.

It is as if Paul opens his heart and mind and gives us a glimpse into his eternal perspective. Every time I read this passage, I am personally convicted. We find here Paul's three primary life objectives; his goals, if you will. What does he want to accomplish the rest of his life?

## Objective #1: That I may win Christ and be found in Him

The word *win* in v. 8 is a verb; the noun form of the same Greek word is used also in v. 7. It is the word *gain*. What does it mean to *win* or *gain* Christ? Vine says it is "So practically appropriating Christ to oneself that He becomes the dominating power in and over one's whole being and circumstances." This is obviously not a salvation statement (in the sense of justification); it is a sanctification statement. At what point do you, dear believer, *win* Christ? At what point are you *found in Him* (v. 9)? At the Judgment Seat, if you indeed appropriate Him consistently in this life here and now, so that He becomes your all-in-all, then you will be *found in Him*.

What is the prerequisite to reaching this goal? The answer is found in v. 7 — by counting all else as loss. By literally considering your personal goals and ambitions and pursuits and accomplishments as dung, as nothing of importance (v. 8). It is a spirit that forsakes the mundane so that Christ can be won. It is a back seat for our plans and desires, so that the far-surpassing greater benefit of knowing Christ can be in the forefront. It is being willing to suffer the loss of all things so that we might win Christ. That is not the way most Christians live in the twenty-first century!

Paul wanted to be found *in Him*. He is not referring to that aspect of salvation, which places believers, positionally, in Christ. He is speaking in a practical sanctification sense. We must learn to live every day of our lives with Christ in the forefront, recognizing that that can never happen of any supposed inherent righteousness on our part, but through the righteous One who lives within us. Jesus is our provision. Again, we think of Gal. 2:20.

I think this first objective is much like what Jesus said on one occasion in the Gospels.

> Verily, verily, I say unto you, Except a corn of wheat fall into the ground and die, it abideth alone: but if it die, it bringeth forth much fruit. He that loveth his life shall lose it; and he that hateth his life in this world shall keep it unto life eternal. John 12:24-25

This is Paul's first goal, stated in a little different way, and it results in gaining Christ and being found *in Him*. It's not a positional standing as *in Him*. It's a practical, experiential being found *in Him*. It is the idea of abiding in the vine, as delineated in John 15.

## Objective #2: That I might attain unto the out-resurrection

This cannot be referring merely to the rapture. The rapture is guaranteed for all saints (1 Thess. 4:13-18). This resurrection is something that Paul hoped to *attain*. The word means to reach or arrive at by striving. It is conditional, not unconditional like the rapture. What could this mean? The important clue is found in the Greek word behind the English word *resurrection*. It is a compound Greek word, not meaning merely resurrection (Greek, *anastasis*), but out-resurrection (Greek, *exanastasis*). It is used only here in the New Testament. It is the idea of rising up from among the resurrected — a resurrection out from amongst those who have been resurrected.

I believe what Paul is longing for is the privilege of being one of those Christ chooses to rule and reign with Him. For many are called (saved), but few are chosen (that is, chosen to rule, chosen to be given the status of firstborn sons — Matt. 22:14). Those who are deemed *firstborn* at the Judgment Seat will apparently be caught away from amongst all the raptured saints to go up to the heavenly Jerusalem, the city of reward, where they will rule with Christ in His kingdom. Instead of being merely earthly subjects in the kingdom, as will be the case with those saints who are wicked and slothful servants, these faithful ones will be caught up into the heavenly Jerusalem and given wonderful privileges, the greatest of which is the presence of Christ.

Sadly, dispensational Christianity has largely assumed all saints will have these privileges by default, because of their positional righteousness in Christ. But that is incorrect, as we have emphasized repeatedly throughout this book. Only those who choose to put on the practical robes of righteousness by appropriating the provision of Christ, will be rewarded in that way. Paul's longing desire is to qualify for this status in the heavenlies. In v. 12 he avoids presumption by saying, "I have not obtained it yet. I am not perfect; that is, I have not reached the final goal of sanctification." So he keeps following Jesus so that he might *apprehend*, that is, lay hold of complete sanctification. Paul wants to take possession (i.e., to obtain the inheritance) in the city of reward. Like Abraham, Paul is looking for the city which hath foundations, whose builder and maker is God.

What is the prerequisite to reaching this goal and obtaining this privilege? According to v. 10, the ticket into the city of reward is suffering. Enduring your trials with the same spirit that Christ endured His. As we noted in an earlier chapter, Rom. 8:17 says we become joint-heirs with Christ if we suffer with Him. Only then will we be glorified together with Him. 2 Tim. 2:12 says, *If we suffer, we shall also reign with him: if we deny him, he also will deny us.* The word *suffer* in the Timothy passage is typically translated *endure* in the New Testament. It is the idea of bearing up under pressure, continuing faithful in your walk with Jesus, come what may. Does that describe you?

## Objective #3: That I might be granted the prize of the up-calling

Again, this high calling is not merely referring to the rapture, nor is it eternity in Heaven. This is a conditional reward for those who are deemed worthy of it. We know that's the case because Paul describes his need to *press* toward this prize. To press is the idea of pursuing. Christians don't need to pursue the rapture. But we must pursue the prize of the up-calling. The word *high* is the idea of something that is upward, it is on high. It is not given to everyone, only to those who are called up to it. Again we think of the out-resurrection mentioned earlier.

But I think there is something more here. He refers to it as the prize of the up-calling of God in Christ Jesus. It seems Paul is longing to be in a special place of close eternal fellowship that is granted only to those who qualify — in the very presence of Christ Himself. I believe that is what Jesus is referring to in John 14:1-6:

> Let not your heart be troubled: ye believe in God, believe also in me. In my Father's house are many mansions: if it were not so, I would have told you. I go to prepare a place for you. And if I go and prepare a place for you, I will come again, and receive you unto myself; that where I am, there ye may be also. And whither I go ye know, and the way ye know. Thomas saith unto him, Lord, we know not whither thou goest; and how can we know the way? Jesus saith unto him, I am the way, the truth, and the life: no man cometh unto the Father, but by me.

The tendency is to interpret these verses as referring to the way of salvation from eternal condemnation and the benefit of eternity in Heaven for all believers. However, that doesn't seem to fit the context. Jesus is speaking to His disciples in the upper room on the eve of His crucifixion. Over the course of several chapters (John 13-17), He has an endearing time of discipleship training with these men. He is reminding them of the special place of fellowship with Christ in the heavenly Jerusalem to which they can aspire — inclusion in the city of reward. Jesus is the ultimate prize to be won, so to speak. We long to be in His presence, but not all saints will be in His immediate presence in the kingdom.

What is the prerequisite to fulfilling this objective? It is twofold. First, forgetting those things that are behind (v. 13). Things like past personal accomplishments. Things like past failures and sins that have been confessed and forsaken. The second prerequisite is reaching forth (the word literally means "stretching") to those things that are out ahead, still future. Pressing toward the mark. This involves a deliberate choice to lay everything else aside in order to accomplish the greater goal — the prize of intimacy with Christ, forever in His presence. Paul said it another way in 1 Cor. 9:24-27:

> Know ye not that they which run in a race run all, but one receiveth the prize? So run, that ye may obtain. And every man that striveth for the mastery is temperate in all things. Now they do it to obtain a corruptible crown; but we an incorruptible. I therefore so run, not as uncertainly; so fight I, not as one that beateth the air: But I keep under my body, and bring it into subjection: lest that by any means, when I have preached to others, I myself should be a castaway.

Notice the intensity of the passage, all the action verbs. What is required for winning the race? Running, striving, temperance (self-control), keeping under the body, bringing into subjection. For what purpose? Lest we become rejected. What a tragedy it would be to become rejected at the Judgment Seat, unfit for rule. If Paul was concerned about the possibility of becoming a castaway, how much more should we?

At the end of his passionate outcry about qualifying for rewards, Paul adds an admonition.

> Let us therefore, as many as be perfect, be thus minded: and if in any thing ye be otherwise minded, God shall reveal even this unto you. Phil. 3:15

The word *perfect* is the idea of maturity and going all the way to the end goal of sanctification with Christ. It is similar to the word Jesus used on the cross, when He cried, *It is finished!* The will of the Father had been accomplished. The goal had been reached. Perfection is not sinlessness. No Christian will ever become sinless this side of eternity. Perfection is the ultimate goal of sanctification, going all the way in discipleship. Paul is challenging us, "If you want to become perfect (go all the way) in your sanctification so that you are rewarded at the Judgment Seat, you should have these three objectives also! And if you don't care about these things, then God can reveal that to you."

Are your objectives for life in line with Phil. 3? Do you have otherworldly ambitions? Or are yours merely worldly? There is much at stake.

# Scripture Index

## Revelation